NONLOCAL NATURE:
THE EIGHT CIRCUITS
OF CONSCIOUSNESS

Some Other Titles From New Falcon Publications

Aha! The Sevenfold Mystery of the Ineffable Love — **By Aleister Crowley**
Bio-Etheric Healing — **By Trudy Lanitis**
Undoing Yourself With Energized Meditation and Other Devices
Secrets of Western Tantra: The Sexuality of the Middle Path
Dogma Daze — **By Christopher S. Hyatt, Ph.D.**
Rebels & Devils; The Psychology of Liberation **Edited by Christopher S. Hyatt, Ph.D.**
Aleister Crowley's Illustrated Goetia
Taboo: Sex, Religion & Magick
Sex Magic, Tantra & Tarot: The Way of the Secret Lover
 — **By Christopher S. Hyatt, Ph.D., and Lon Milo DuQuette**
Pacts With The Devil
Urban Voodoo: A Beginner's Guide to Afro-Caribbean Magic
 — **By Jason Black and Christopher S. Hyatt, Ph.D.**
The Psychopath's Bible — **By Christopher S. Hyatt, Ph.D., and Jack Willis**
Ask Baba Lon — **By Lon Milo DuQuette**
Aleister Crowley and the Treasure House of Images **By J.F.C. Fuller, Aleister Crowley, Lon Milo DuQuette and Nancy Wasserman**
Enochian World of Aleister Crowley **By Lon Milo DuQuette and Aleister Crowley**

Info-Psychology   Neuropolitique   The Game of Life
What Does WoMan Want? — **By Timothy Leary, Ph.D.**

Be Yourself - A Guide to Relaxation and Health
Dr. Israel Regardie's Definitive Work on Aleister Crowley, The Eye In The Triangle
Healing Energy, Prayer and Relaxation
My Rosicrucian Adventure
Teachers of Fulfillment
The Complete Golden Dawn System of Magic
The Eye in the Triangle: An Interpretation of Aleister Crowley
The Golden Dawn Audio CDs
The Legend of Aleister Crowley
The Portable Complete Golden Dawn System of Magic
The Tree of Life
What You Should Know About the Golden Dawn — **By Dr. Israel Regardie**

Roll Away The Stone/The Herb Dangerous **By Israel Regardie and Aleister Crowley**

Rebellion, Revolution and Religiousness — **By Osho**
Reichian Therapy: A Practical Guide for Home Use — **By Dr. Jack Willis**
Woman's Orgasm: A Guide to Sexual Satisfaction — **By Benjamin Graber, M.D., and Georgia Kline-Graber, R.N.**
Shaping Formless Fire   Seizing Power   Taking Power — **By Stephen Mace**
The Illuminati Conspiracy: The Sapiens System — **By Donald Holmes, M.D.**
The Secret Inner Order Rituals of the Golden Dawn — **By Pat Zalewski**

MANY OF OUR TITLES AVAILABLE ON KINDLE!
Please visit our website at http://www.newfalcon.com

NONLOCAL NATURE: THE EIGHT CIRCUITS OF CONSCIOUSNESS

By James A. Heffernan

NEW FALCON PUBLICATIONS
LAS VEGAS, NEVADA, U.S.A.

Copyright © 2017 James A. Heffernan

All rights reserved. No part of this book,
in part or in whole, may be reproduced, transmitted,
or utilized, in any form or by any means, electronic or mechanical,
including photocopying, recording, or by any information storage
and retrieval system, without permission in writing
from the publisher, except for brief quotations
in critical articles, books and reviews.

ISBN 13: 978-1-56184-541-5
ISBN 10: 1-56184-541-8

First New Falcon Publications Edition 2017

The paper used in this publication meets the minimum requirements
of the American National Standard for Permanence of
Paper for Printed Library Materials Z39.48-1984

Printed in USA

NEW FALCON PUBLICATIONS
9550 South Eastern Avenue • Suite 253
Las Vegas, NV 89123
www.newfalcon.com
email: info@newfalcon.com

DEDICATED

to the memory of Robert Anton Wilson

Vivat spiritus

TABLE OF CONTENTS

INTRODUCTION	1
OVERVIEW	5
CIRCUIT 1	21
CIRCUIT 2	33
CIRCUIT 3	43
CIRCUIT 4	57
EXPLORATION	71
CIRCUIT 5	103
CIRCUIT 6	115
THE NOOSPHERE	125
CIRCUIT 7	133
CIRCUIT 8	155
THE IMPLICATE ORDER	169
TO CONCLUDE	179
APPENDIX	181
ABOUT THE AUTHOR	183

INTRODUCTION

*"Atomicity is a common property of the
Within and the Without of things."*
—de Chardin

This book, which I am glad you have found, is about, and inspired by, the Eight Circuit Model of Consciousness. This working model was first formulated by Dr. Timothy Leary, and later expanded upon by philosophers Robert Anton Wilson (RAW) and Antero Alli. Their work has been invaluable to me over the years, and without it, the present work would never have existed. The framework these gentlemen have pioneered is the most general and most fundamental schematic for human consciousness that I have ever encountered. It outlines the basic neurological circuits which constitute the nervous system—of humans, of mammals, indeed of all sentient creatures to some degree or other. In this way, it is very general, and also serves to highlight the kinship that all Earth organisms—and potentially those of other planets as well—share, as we all exhibit, at least in part, a common continuum. This enables us to negotiate terrestrial affairs, and to exist meaningfully as beings in a universe that represents one undivided, flowing movement—one in which we are all participants.

The difficulty with presenting ideas like the ones in this book is that they are quite challenging to a lot of people. Indeed, it is here postulated that most people, most of the time, are on a kind of "auto-pilot" in their thoughts and behaviors—that they are essentially quasi-deterministic robots. Precisely those people have no inkling of this, and to suggest it would engender anger, criticism, or worse. This book is all about becoming less robotic, but in doing so, we have to face the fact that ordinarily, we have very little control over ourselves. Activating higher and higher circuits on the tree can be liberating, and it can be painful, but recognizing one's robothood, and understanding that the truth is far richer than the dreariness to which too many of us are accustomed, is the first step in opening doors that truly can transform our lives for the better. It is also desirable to achieve a familiarity with the inner workings of nature, which a certain awareness, deeply tied to the dynamics of the present subject, enables one over time to gain.

It must be stressed that we are not robots. We are beings, who fundamentally and truly exist, and we live in a sea of awareness, of which our "selves" are localized, concentrated whirlpools. The higher circuits, which exist in everyone, and with which anyone can learn to gain facility, embody the dynamics of this awareness, which is not deterministic and classical, but mind-like and quantum. As one gets farther along, this metamorphosis from the Aristotelian, Newtonian paradigm into the non-linear, relativistic, nonlocal one can be more and more viscerally felt, until one finally cries "Aha!" and it all makes sense. More than anything with this book I hope to make sense to you, the reader, and if I do, my task has been a fruitful one.

Right off the bat I shall give an overview of each circuit of the nervous system, ascending from the first through the eighth. That should prime the reader with the basic ideas that unfold in the developing portions of the book. I shall then go into a bit more philosophical depth regarding each circuit in turn, with an exploratory section in the middle, and two intercalary sections I felt were necessary for a proper elucidation of the principles—one on the noosphere, and one on the implicate order. All this will be followed by a brief concluding note and an appendix—for anyone interested—containing a thought experiment titled "A Quantum Mechanical Interpretation of the Eight Circuit Model."

The words I have quoted above convey a powerful reflection of one of the primary themes of this book. I'll leave it to the reader to discover for herself just what it all means, but suffice it to say that "atomicity"—a clear reference to the atomic circuit which makes up the ultimate level of the schema presented in this book—does indeed exist as a property both of that which is *within*, and that which is *without*. It is hoped that one will find that there are not in fact two categories here, but only one.

OVERVIEW

Circuit 1: The Oral Bio-Survival Circuit

This circuit first evolved on Earth some 3-4 billion years ago, and is the first circuit activated when an infant is born. It programs perception into an either-or linear function which is divided into that which is nurturing, helpful, beneficial and *safe*—what is to be positively approached—and that which is noxious, toxic, harmful and *dangerous*—what is to be avoided, fled from or attacked. There is here a *forward-back* orientation: advance, go forward, sniff, touch, taste, bite; or retreat, back off, flee, escape.

The imprinting of this circuit creates the basic configuration or template of trust and suspicion which, unless re-imprinted, will last for life. It also identifies the external stimuli which will set the approach-avoidance patterns for the rest of one's life. Some have an imprint that clings to the familiar, some have an imprint that seeks novelty and exploration of new places, and most are somewhere in between. This hard-wired infantile information and behavior system forms the foundation of, and essentially dictates the course of, all of the circuits on top of it, almost always without the knowledge or awareness of the conscious ego. When a gun is pointed at you, whatever action you take will be accompanied by the feeling later on that "I just found myself doing it," as the ancient reptilian response is automatic and reflexive.

For humans, the primary first circuit object, and the stimulus leading to our first imprint, is the mother's breast. As an infant, we take nourishment from mother's nipples/breasts and judge objects by putting them in our mouths. This is the Oral Stage of Freud. The happiest areas of the bio-survival system—imprinted by the safety and security around mommy—can only be "remembered" or re-experienced with certain chemicals that trigger neurotransmitters similar to those activated during breastfeeding. Opiates serve this function for too many.

This circuit gives rise to the "screen" and sense of awareness that we colloquially refer to as consciousness. For example, when anesthetized, first circuit awareness is shut down and doctors may perform surgery without one's wishing or attempting to flee.

In vertebrate organisms, we can see the priority of first circuit functions firsthand. All survival and sensory equipment is located in the front of the organism—mouth, eyes, ears, nose. The nervous system is clearly oriented toward the perceptibility of what is safe or dangerous, while very little is happening neurologically in the rear. Fish are the prime example of this stage of evolution.

Circuit 2: The Anal-Emotional-Territorial Circuit

This circuit formed around 500 million years ago as vertebrates appeared and began competing for territory. This tunnel reality is activated in humans when the transition from crawling to walking is made at the time of the toddling stage. This is why we have the phrase, "He or she is acting like a two year old." There is a distinct *up-down* orientation on this circuit: rear up, swell the body to appear as large as possible, growl, roar, bark, howl, shriek; or shrink, drop tail between legs, murmur, skulk, crawl, yelp. These are all, of course, *dominance-submission* signals.

Mammalian politics is the direct result of second circuit activity. Human politicians are adept at speaking to the *emotions* of the humans whose support they want; emotions of course constitute the essence of the power-territory dynamics endemic to all mammalian packs, and all emotion relates to one's perception of whether one's personal territory (and power) has been supported, violated, augmented or reduced, which in humans can get extremely abstract. This system is predominant in those whose lives center around power; it is latent and usually only emerges in conflict situations in most others.

Indeed, political group behavior exhibits this circuit most ridiculously in displays of mammalian pack-solidarity such as attacking, verbally or otherwise, a rival pack; and swelling the body and making howling noises—which make up the usual domination signals among birds, reptiles, mammals and politicians. This is of course directly related to the phenomenon of the "alpha male."

As with the first circuit, whatever imprint is made on this circuit remains, except in very rare circumstances, constant for life. It identifies the stimuli which will trigger behaviors that are dominant/aggressive, submissive/cooperative, or at a point somewhere in between. Someone who tends to behave emotionally or egotistically is someone who has disproportionate activity on this circuit. This circuit is, indeed, the foundational basis of all ego and all emotion.

Those who take a strong, dominant imprint on this circuit seek positions of power and control all their lives; those with a submissive imprint seek dominant types to lead them, and most people settle somewhere between these extremes. There exists a masochist stance toward those people above one in the hierarchy (the government, landlords, bosses, etc.), and a sadist stance toward those below (wives, children, "inferior" races, the poor, etc.).

Whenever real danger appears, there is a full reversion to the bio-survival circuit. This occurs when there is a threat to life rather than merely to status. The aftermath of any confrontation usually reinforces boundaries, and here we have the phenomenon of excretions, which any dog owner can understand. All mammals mark their territories with excretions; during the toddling stage for humans, toilet training occurs, so we have a mutual reinforcement of anality around the imprinting stage of this circuit. This is the Anal Stage of Freud.

There is more *time* on this circuit; exploring a dominance hierarchy and its power signals goes more slowly than first circuit attacking or fleeing, which seems to happen instantly. The emotional dimension of time is dilated compared to the instantaneous nature of first circuit phenomena.

The second circuit can be imprinted for some territoriality, much territoriality, or no territoriality at all—depending on ecological necessity. As always, the picture is far from simple. But the picture that has been outlined has the benefit of empirical support, coherence and elegance. And as Lieutenant Commander Spock reminds us, "Insults are effective only when emotion is present."

Circuit 3: The Rational-Semantic-Manual Circuit

This circuit, which we usually refer to as the "mind," formed approximately 4-5 million years ago when hominins began to separate from other primates. It has its roots in the Paleolithic, and is the basis for the dissemination of all subsequent human culture, via language, which was made possible through the development of self-reflective, symbolic thought. It is activated in humans when the young child begins handling artifacts and sending and receiving laryngeal signals, a.k.a. human speech. The signals which are received, processed and transmitted at this level mediate the activity of the hands and the muscles of the larynx. There is a distinct *left-right* orientation here, arising from the interplay of the dexterous hands and their role in manipulating artifacts, which develops alongside learning how to speak and think.

An imprint toward "cleverness"—meaning dexterous and articulate—or "dumb"—meaning clumsy in speech and/or symbolic thinking—can be made depending on the quality of the environment, and usually lasts a lifetime. If one is rational and articulate, one has had a favorable imprint, and it must be added that genetics surely play a large role here. If one is dull and unremarkable, they have had bad luck, bad genes, or some combination of the two. Though we tend to think of intelligence as a purely genetic phenomenon, the random vicissitudes of one's social, economic and cultural environments, as well as one's upbringing, largely determine the imprint one takes, which could be just as consequential as the bare genes one was dealt. Subsequent conditioning and learning all occur within the parameters of this original imprint, which can be fluent (well-spoken and clear-thinking), dull (inarticulate and unthinking), or any place in between, which is where we find the majority of people.

This system allows for "time-binding"—signals can cross eons of time, e.g. the ideas of the ancients, or the Buddha, Jesus, etc. Moreover, signals in the present have the potential to reach the distant future. Thus symbolic thinking enables problem solving with the thought of many time periods at its disposal. Indeed, culture as we know it would be totally impossible without this time-binding function. This circuit then allows us to create mathematical systems, which in turn give rise to all of science; we were enabled in the past to predict phenomena before the technology existed to measure those phenomena. We can build complex machines, which further transform the third circuit in a positive-feedback loop.

In large part, the reality-tunnels pertaining to this circuit enable extremes of creativity to be reached; art, writing, science, poetry, music, engineering, film, etc., could not be possible without creative impulses bursting through the neural highways making up this circuit. And these neural highways would have no systems of reasoning, philosophy or tradition without the time-binding function. After a certain period of development of this circuit, the individual can begin, with his mature cognitive mind, to integrate, organize, synthesize symbols intelligently and can even invent or create novel configurations of symbols and artifacts. We sometimes call such activity "creativity" or "independent thought."

There is more *time* on this circuit than on the first or second, even enough to posit various theories about time. Without an ample, unhurried timeframe in which to operate, theories like Newtonian mechanics or relativity—two theories about time itself—would be impossible. Couple that with the time-bound systems reaching us from thousands of years in the past, and time is a very central feature of the third circuit universe, indeed. One rule of thumb to remember when thinking about this circuit: Thought is largely internal speech. This fact underscores the development and fundamental operation of this system, which can continue learning and growing for life.

Circuit 4: The "Moral"-Social-Sexual Circuit

This neurological circuit seems to have appeared in humans around 150-200,000 years ago, when anatomically modern man fully evolved, though certainly there were proto-versions of love-sensation in animals going back quite a ways, though of course no morality. It is generally activated at puberty when there are the known glandular releases of hormones involved in the metamorphosis to adulthood. The first orgasms or mating experiences imprint the sex-role that a person is likely to exhibit for life. The sex-role of a human is, as RAW has noted, as rote and repetitious as that of any other mammal—or bird or fish or insect. The fourth circuit mediates signals (in concert with the third) that constitute tribal and ethnic culture that spans eons, and introduces more fully than the previous three circuits the subjective dimension of *time*.

At puberty, DNA signals are sent that it is now time for mating; the body metamorphoses, and the mind changes radically as well, generating a whole new "self" that will interact with and interpret the world. As usual, imprinting and genetics play the lion's share of the role, with conditioning and learning modifying but seldom radically altering the gene-imprint imperatives. If the environment provides a positive sex imprint, sexual health and even joy are likely to be the norm for life; if the environment provides a negative sex imprint, sex is likely to be a source of pain and disturbance for life. Very unfortunately, many millions exhibit the latter, and also very unfortunately, re-imprinting technology—which, without sanctions, would be an inevitable development in psychology and psychiatry—is virtually nonexistent. So many of us are stuck as robots powerless to alter our own wiring.

The socio-sexual circuit is just that: it is concerned with operating within and between social networks and interpersonal relationships of all kinds, including friendships. As it appeared with the advent of tribal groups, it deals primarily with moral, social and sexual tribal rules passed down directly over time, and, as mentioned, it has served to cement our perception of time. Oxytocin is the elemental neurotransmitter on this circuit, which can be stimulated in a number of ways, both natural and artificial. Tribal morality is what governs this circuit, and in practice, sexual deviation is how it is usually expressed. No one acts quite the way the established moral codes would prefer, but everyone pretends this is not the case. Hence the ubiquitous proliferation of *guilt* felt by so very many humans. There is a way to transcend this guilt, and we shall move on to that arena presently.

Circuit 5: The Holistic Neurosomatic Circuit

As the soul begins to reclaim itself, this is the first of the "higher" circuits, which is usually not highly active in most humans, but which lays the groundwork for post-Euclidean perceptions. It involves the perception of an energized and more conscious body, and reveals the inherent connectedness of body and mind through neurological and somatic feedback. Here we transition from a linear, visual space to a richer, deeper sensory space. The opening and imprinting of this circuit is under the purview of Tantric shamans, Hatha yogis and psychonauts, and quite possibly the reader. It can be activated by sensory deprivation, social isolation, psychological stress or severe shock, as well as surfing, skiing, snowboarding, diving, and a liberal sexual cultural outlook—not to mention cannabis and other psychedelics. It has historically been reserved to the aristocracies and leisure classes, as well as underground occult and secret societies, but in the twentieth century there was the democratization in the sixties of which we are all aware.

With the expanded, energized somatic awareness experienced on the fifth circuit, the natural is beautiful, enhanced somatic function brings intensified pleasure, and normal societal matters seem trivial and dreary compared with the new and wonderful body-consciousness. It seems to be a Zen experience of a kind of rapture wholly unknown to those who have not activated this circuit. The transition from the fourth to the fifth circuit can be problematic because the new awareness and its attendant behaviors are often seen as antisocial. One begins to realize that one's natural bodily sensations are more pleasurable and more interesting than the social game. Mundane affairs are seen to be limited and robotic.

For some, fifth circuit awareness gives rise to the higher circuits beyond it. For some, one remains at this level. And for many who achieve this level of awareness, there is a falling back to the lower circuits, usually due to domestic and professional responsibilities. This is some kind of tragedy, and yet we see it over and over, in each generation. Perhaps when, in the future, we are released from our hive roles by intelligent robots performing the work, there can be a kind of neurosomatic renaissance in a society organized around some locus other than employment. Who knows? I hope so.

Circuit 6: The Neurogenetic-Morphogenetic Circuit

The first scientific model of this circuit appeared in Rupert Sheldrake's *A New Science of Life*. Leary and Grof, just as Jung and Freud did, assumed that certain non-ego information that was being accessed, which was known not to originate in the brain, must be coming from the DNA. Sheldrake, a biologist, knew that the genetic material cannot carry this information. He therefore suggested that some sort of nonlocal field (like those I shall be discussing later) was involved, and he named this the *morphogenetic field*. This field communicates nonlocally between genes, but cannot properly be found *in* the genes. Analogously, Conan O'Brien "travels" between TV sets but cannot be found "in" them. Later on, I shall describe the *noosphere*, a collective information field around the Earth, and how it relates to this circuit. Leary and Wilson call this the "neurogenetic" circuit.

At this level, the nervous system begins to receive signals from within the individual neuron, engaging in a feedback loop between the conscious mind and the genetic material itself, which is engaged in a constant DNA-RNA dialogue. Here one has access to the genetic memory contained in DNA. Historically, certain Hindu groups and later some Sufi sects unraveled many of its secrets, although this log is only available in very esoteric or occult literature, and is therefore not widely acknowledged by those with no access to that material or the experience itself. Many Hindu and Sufi poets gave marvelously accurate and prescient descriptions of evolution thousands of years before Darwin arrived.

Interspecies symbiosis and Gaian ecology, and also as I have noted the noosphere, exist through the widespread network of DNA found on Earth, which is the single greatest and most complex intelligence now operating on the planet. If one tunes into this consciousness, the full complement of the genetic archives becomes accessible. Many people experiencing this circuit speak, rather mystically, of reincarnation, past lives and notions of physical immortality. This circuit's external analogue is the control of DNA itself, which we are seeing through genetic engineering and cloning. This awareness can be activated through advanced yogas, intense numinous experiences and extreme stresses or shocks, and is known to be triggered by certain psychedelic chemicals. If those methods are outside of one's purview, there are excellent books on ecology and genetics available at the local library, and it's always enlightening to go to the zoo with a conscientious and observant attitude. Remember when you do it that, in reality, you're not as different from these creatures as you've been led to believe.

Circuit 7: The Neuroelectric "Metaprogramming" Circuit

At this stage of neurological function, the nervous system becomes aware of its own programming and operation; an awareness of awareness gets generated. Count Korzybski, the semanticist, called this state "consciousness of abstracting"; John Lilly called it "metaprogramming," or in other words, programming one's programming. This circuit operates on the Einsteinian, relativistic level, and one recognizes here that the Euclidean, Aristotelian, Newtonian models or platforms are limited to a certain restricted domain. We know this is the case from physics, but as this awareness unfolds it turns more into a perception than an intellectual realization. Magick and psychedelic chemicals are known to activate this circuit, as well as Raja yoga, and the hermetic manuals of the medieval and Renaissance alchemists and the Illuminati, Knights Templar, etc.

It is very difficult, if not impossible, to communicate meaningful signals from this level to individuals operating on lower circuits; the channel is certain to be filled with noise and misunderstanding. Certain characteristics to be found on circuit 7 are: high velocities, dilated time, relativistic phenomena, fission-fusion shifting of perceptions, spectral (rather than dual) awareness, multiple-choice options, etc. Mammalian politics, and indeed most aspects of mundane reality, are here transcended and seen as trivial, artificial, ultimately wholly unimportant in the face of a much more fundamental and sophisticated reality. Certain telepathic phenomena are associated with this circuit.

An Einsteinian consciousness reveals itself, one which is no longer frozen to the lower circuits or to the body. The neurological reality comprises a relativistic torrent of millions of bio-electric signals flowing through a neural network of 100 billion cells. Biochemical-electrical changes take place at synapse junctions which liberate the flow of signals, which are primarily electrical, from their routine patterns. The static world of imprinting and conditioning dissolves, unveiling a plethora of paths for the mind to take, where in the past only one-at-a-time was available.

Physicists like Henry P. Stapp and Richard Muller point out that the laws of physics do not rule out the possibility of free will, and that from a certain perspective they tend to support the existence of such a phenomenon. Physicists and mathematicians tend to be metaprogrammers, so Stapp and Muller are eminently entitled to their provocative opinions. Perhaps we are not talking about *free* will here, but rather *true* will. These phenomena exist in the arena of metaprogramming.

There has been a very unfortunate suppression and outlawing of scientific research in this area that, if permitted, could lead to potential psychological and psychiatric advancements that could revolutionize the fields. Only now, after almost fifty years, is modest research being done (very quietly) even though psychedelic substances are still strictly scheduled. This is really a new frontier that could very profitably be explored, but society has chosen to throw the scientific baby out with the recreational bath water, unfortunately. It is to be hoped that such ideas as these become less and less arcane sooner rather than later. In the meantime, the true self is available to all.

Circuit 8: The Neuroatomic Nonlocal Quantum Circuit

This circuit, which isn't really a circuit, is infra-, supra-, meta-physiological; it comprises the quantum mechanical information-communication system. Here, spacetime is transcended; mass-energy-electromagnetism is transcended; the speed-of-light-barrier is transcended. Circuit 8 is something akin to DNA and the noosphere's being the planetary "brain"—this circuit is a manifestation of the universe's "brain," like a giant quantum computer into which each individual is plugged. It is triggered by extreme shocks, out-of-body experiences, and high doses of certain chemicals.

Neuroatomic experiences have appeared in the reports of certain yogis, shamans and poets since time immemorial. They are non-spatio-temporal—beyond mind and matter. When one gets to that place, one sees that consciousness pervades existence, so that, in essence, every point in space is like a little eye—like the jeweled net of Indra. Also, with this awareness comes the realization that something like an electron is as much a subjective as it is an objective entity. At this stage, there is no distinction between subject and object.

The metaphysiological quantum intelligence occurs at the level of the ground of nuclear particles and creates or projects mass-energy, arranging atoms in countless complex and coherent patterns, making all chemistry possible as well as everything you see before you. This is an intelligent process, and let it be submitted that there is a kind of nonrandom intelligence governing nature, and possibly leading to the coherence we see in DNA and evolution. We shall touch on the implicate order later on. It seems, at least to some of us, that the popular principle of blind chance is really rather ridiculous from a certain perspective. Astronaut Ed Mitchell, on the surface of the Moon, realized beyond doubt that "life in this universe was not just an accident based on random processes" but that it has "meaning and direction." His "peak experience" on the lunar surface made "the presence of divinity" become "almost palpable." It is eminently possible that astronaut Mitchell activated his higher circuits, and their natural language spoke to him through this peak experience. In any case, such a realization could not come from a more trustworthy human being—one who touched the objective, if only briefly. This conscious, intelligent ground informs all nature, and it is hoped that such an idea will work its way into the reader's consideration, if not his or her soul.

I'd like to make one final point in this overview. *Star Trek* episodes and movies give wonderful depictions of the Eight Circuit Model. Here's a rundown of the basics:

1. Scotty: Engineer responsible for the functioning, safety, and life-support of the ship
2. Dr. McCoy: Emotional and sentimental, he is always trying to get Spock to display feelings
3 Mr. Spock: Science-officer, Vulcan, always operating on a fundamental principle of logic and reason, decrying emotion as irrational and extraneous
4. Captain Kirk: Alternately paternalistic and romantic, with a morality based upon the safety of his ship and crew

They all regularly make contact with circuit 5-8 intelligences throughout the galaxy. Some of their circuit 8 contacts are particularly interesting, many involving a kind of nonlocal telepathy. Your homework: Watch an episode of *Star Trek* and apply the present hypothesis to it. It will make a lot of sense!

CIRCUIT 1

First Circuit Function

The specific stimulus which activates each neuro-umbilical survival system imprint, as Leary calls it, is determined purely by chance—by environmental accident. Whatever external factors are present during the sensitive period will be imprinted, for good or ill. Given the fundamental causality which imprint systems have over the human nervous system, most people would feel rather embarrassed to compare such facts to their own conceptions of self, ego and conscious choice/free will. Human beings are largely robots programmed and directed by these neural imprints which trigger standardized patterns of discharge in a particular environmental scenario, and which really have their basis in accidentally seared patterns.

Shortly after birth, when the trauma has subsided, the baby's nervous system "takes a picture," focusing every bit of the sensory apparatus on the soft, warm, milk-producing stimulus of the breast. It permanently photographs this picture as safe and beneficial for survival. If this viscerotonic imprint is not made because of absence of the appropriate stimulus during the critical period, the basic survival and security system does not get properly and effectively wired-up, which often leads to negative childhood manifestations such as autism or schizophrenia.

Biosurvival language tends to be global across species: The movements and sounds which indicate "I am safe" or "you are safe" are recognized by almost all animals regardless of ecosystem or culture. Behaviors which express pain or fear of physical threat are also generally recognized and essentially terrestrially universal. Applicable actions are eating, vomiting, sucking, embracing, moaning and other vocalizations, showing disgust, and especially physical aggression or menace. The first circuit is quite generally expressed.

The circuit is imprinted by the mother or mother substitute and conditioned by subsequent nurturing or threat. It involves sucking, feeding, cuddling and bodily safety and security. It retreats—quite mechanically—from what is perceived to be noxious, predatory or in any way dangerous. Anything in any way associated with these dangers, via imprint and conditioning, is to be avoided.

Behaviors

The range of behaviors that can potentially be imprinted is vast. As RAW tells us, there is a story of a baby giraffe who, in the absence of a mother who was accidentally killed by a Jeep shortly after its birth, imprinted the Jeep instead! He followed it around, made vocalizations toward it, attempted to suckle from it and later on tried to mate with it. He also mentions the episode related by Konrad Lorenz, who witnessed a goose's behavior after it apparently imprinted a ping-pong ball. It spent its entire adult life attempting to mount ping-pong balls, utterly indifferent to the presence of female geese.

This first circuit imprint is the first, and perhaps most behaviorally fundamental, of all developmental steps in terran organisms. It stipulates the criteria for going forward to approach the safe and nourishing, and going back, to avoid the threatening and predatory. This is crucial not only for the health and safety of every organism, but also for all subsequent imprints, which are functionally built within the parameters of the first. But that is a bit of a digression. Any mammal, for example, takes an imprint on the first circuit from the first bio-survival object it encounters. For the giraffe, it was a Jeep, but for most creatures, it is usually the teat. In this way, DNA has programmed us to seek a comfortable, safe zone around a mothering organism. In the absence of a mother, a four-legged giraffe may imprint a four-wheeled Jeep, and a round, white goose might fixate upon a round, white ping-pong ball. Evolution is subtle and brilliant, but we all know it isn't perfect.

Bio-survival and oral activity (or fixations) are deeply interlinked. Dogs experience intense pleasure while chewing on a bone. This is not merely idle activity, but the result of positive neurotransmitters being released due to first circuit stimulation.

(Neurotransmitters are special molecules which attach to the circuits of the brain at junctions called synapses and which alter its electrical, chemical and colloidal properties, thereby changing the brain's function and the content of consciousness. They are literally brain-change chemicals.) We also see many oral fixations in humans, particularly nail-biting, gum-chewing, snacking excessively, smoking, etc. This is not meaningless behavior but reflects a strong and perhaps less than balanced imprint on this circuit.

Past and Present

This circuit appeared, in primitive form, along with the first organisms almost four billion years ago. In humans, it is associated with the autonomic (involuntary) nervous system, and is interconnected with the endocrine system and of course the brain. This circuit is unhealthy, i.e. harbors some form of pathology or dysfunction, in perhaps ninety percent of the population. This is unacceptable, but is a necessary consequence of living in a profoundly sick society. This also highlights the degree to which the vast majority of the population is robotized. A person who is riddled with anxiety, as so many in the modern age are, will not be able to calmly and impartially make careful observations, judgments or decisions very readily, and therefore must be on some form of awful, fearful autopilot—unaware of very much that is going on around them, or even within them. And so the masses slumber.

Chance

This is a particularly mechanical circuit. That is, behaviors associated with it are very rapid and quite automatic. Decision-making has nothing to do with it. One is not conscious of time at all when acting or reacting here. At the slightest provocation, a dog will start to bark and raise its hackles immediately, automatically. It is not until after this first circuit function is fulfilled that the dog begins to consciously evaluate the situation. Humans are not much different. When some stimulus causes us to become intensely fearful, we react without even knowing we are doing it, and it goes without saying that we don't think about our reaction. Traumatic episodes are remembered very differently than a stroll in the park, or a conversation with a pretty girl.

All of the imprints we are discussing are made utterly and totally by chance. The circumstances surrounding the period of imprint vulnerability, which are governed only by happenstance, are what determine the type of imprint an individual will take, and be subject to for the rest of his life. All sorts of traits can be imprinted: inquisitiveness, timidity, confidence, neurotic tendencies, bravery, cowardice, intrepidity, fear, involvement, withdrawal, extroversion, introversion, etc. These random imprints lay the basis for totally robotic reactions to various stimuli; it is only through much tribulation that one may later come to learn how to reprogram one's neural circuits, and become, maybe not totally free, but at least less robotic. Most people will, tragically, never acquire the skill and opportunity to be able to do so.

Bio-Survival Substitutes

In addition to imprints we have both genetics and conditioning as fundamentally important factors. These factors allow the individual to transition from identifying the space around mommy as safe toward regarding the larger family and the tribe as objects of safety and protection as well. Some time after civilization took off, this configuration was no longer tenable. The tribe became so large, and society so different from humanity's natural niche, that we had to hook our bio-survival drives onto more and more abstract substitutes. Examples of such objects included property, especially cultivated land and livestock, and money. Through the evolution of history, and through concurrent conditioning over time, money is now the principal instrument for bio-survival, and it is no wonder that it is at the center of just about everybody's consciousness. If, in RAW's words, those green "tickets" are withdrawn, acute first circuit anxiety appears immediately and forcefully. Our minds are fixated, understandably, on winning and keeping these tickets.

Humans in their evolutionary setting were directly personally bonded, or meaningfully acquainted, with a few dozen people, and this was the social unit in which our species is meant, biologically, to exist. In the modern state, things are very different, and all sorts of weird phenomena emerge. A healthy first circuit milieu is absent, so we have to fill it in with substitutes and this leads to some of the big existential problems we face; the anomie, loneliness and isolation of modern America, and perhaps the Western world, is a result of very basic bio-survival needs and genetic expectations not being met. There are other factors involved in our general dysfunction beyond the scope of the current subject which could take up several volumes, but suffice it to say that some of the pathology, like extreme anxiety, fear, paranoia, loneliness, opiate addiction, etc., arises because we are connecting our first circuits to unnatural and toxic situations (and chemicals) with which they were never meant to function. Those notorious green tickets are at the center of all this, creating the hot mess that is modern civilization. With our current socioeconomic makeup, bio-survival anxiety, which afflicts the majority of those now on this planet, can only disappear when everyone attains enough tickets. This is, as many would agree, a lofty and improbable to reach goal. With the new and revolutionary factor concerning automation and artificial intelligence, we should expect unemployment to go nowhere but up. Perhaps a Universal Basic Income will be required to keep society from drifting into dystopia, and perhaps such a thing might end or curtail the aforementioned problems. But we have a very rocky road ahead from here to there, and bio-survival insecurity is going to remain with us for many years to come. It makes one wonder what our purported "freedom" really is.

Play

The phenomenon of play is deeply tied to first circuit function. We are wired to play with our own bodies, the bodies of others, and the environment, if it is friendly. Playfulness is a very healthy trait, and in those who do not do it, because of timidity, shame, fear, or what have you, more often than not some type of pathology develops. Such a lack of playfulness is generally the result of a negative imprint taken on this circuit, in which the universe is experienced as hostile, frightening or dangerous, and this is accompanied by a lifelong tendency for all perceptions to fit into the unfortunate personal map or reality-tunnel that this off-balance imprint has generated. People who are affected by this unhealthy first circuit dysfunction often assume extreme ideological roles, like fundamentalism, right- or left-wing politics, racism, sexism, etc. When one lives in a universe essentially of fear and distrust, it is unsurprising that such imbalances in feeling and thinking are often the result.

Automatic Reactions

As has been stated previously, the first circuit is the most fundamental circuit for the organism, and largely for that reason, the most automatic. Bio-survival circuit reactions are never thought out, are never weighed and considered, if for no other reason than simply because there is not enough *time*. Time is not a factor here, and is never really part of a bio-survival perception. Everything happens all-at-once, and a traumatic or harmful episode is never thought about until well after one has reacted to it. Second and third circuit rationalizations always come later. If gazelles had to think every time a lion approached or attacked, they would go extinct as the time it would take to do so would ensure the lion's quick victory. Since gazelles are not extinct, we can reasonably say that their first circuits are working properly—that is, quickly and automatically, without any hesitation or lengthy consideration.

When the bio-survival circuit kicks into gear, all other mental activity ceases—all of the other circuits shut down until the potentially dangerous situation has been satisfactorily dealt with. The functioning of this circuit is the most behaviorally robotic aspect of all living organisms. For humans, it is worth noting that bio-survival functions are *pre-verbal*, and are therefore, for us, by definition not in the province of thought—more felt or sensed than considered. First circuit reactions are also felt all over the body, instantly—another aspect of its robotic, knee-jerk nature. Many schools of bio-survival therapy know that they must work on the body—especially the breathing—first and foremost, to deal with bad imprints. To try to reason it out, like a psychiatrist might, can accomplish nothing here.

Basis for Life

The evolution of the bio-survival circuit originated what we generally consider "consciousness." The terminology is loose here, but in other words, the "screen" that displays our inner show of the reality around us evolved in order to secure nourishment and safety, as without any sort of awareness of the environment this would have been impossible. From humans to bonobos to platypi to rattlesnakes, this movie "screen" or inner show is what enables us to survive, whether it be given by light, heat, smell or what have you. When a human goes in for surgery, the anesthesiologist shuts off, with chemicals, this screen and the first circuit itself, so that the surgeon may engage in radical traumatization of the patient's tissues without the patient's needing to cry out and flee. Truly, without this circuit as a basis for life, none of the others could ever have evolved.

We shall next move on to a discussion of the anal-emotional-territorial circuit, which expands the survival functions of the organism, but exists very much within the parameters of the first circuit, which as has been noted, is the most fundamental and is the one which has the first say in dealing with any new situation. We turn now to circuit 2.

CIRCUIT 2

Emotional Politics

The second circuit, which we are dubbing anal-emotional-territorial, first appeared significantly among vertebrates some 500 million years ago, and has reached its most complex development in mammals—which of course includes humans. It modulates bio-social *power* in all its sundry forms. In humans, this circuit first comes into play at the onset of the "toddling" stage of infant development. Walking about, negotiating physical objects and obstacles and especially learning to manipulate others are key functions of this circuit, and some combination of these is usually what triggers an imprint, which paves the way for subsequent conditioning. Depending on environmental accidents (as all neurological imprints do), this circuit will impart a strong, dominant role, a weak submissive role, or one at any point in between (as most people exist at neither extreme). This sort of behavior is perhaps most easily observed in dogs.

The central reflex, indicating authority or dominance, on the second circuit is to swell the muscles or raise the hackles, and scream or howl or yelp or roar. The central submission reflex is to shrink the muscles, lower the head, place tail between legs and slink away. As RAW noted, "You will find this among dogs, primates, fowl and employees who wish to keep their jobs everywhere." This circuit processes the rules, emotional dynamics and pecking order of the local territory. This is the Anal Stage in Freudian psychology.

Second Circuit Dynamics

Gestures, postures and verbalizations which communicate a status or territorial defense message are almost universally recognized. This applies quite generally across the mammalian kingdom. In human societies, we easily see that gestures indicating affiliation, dominance, submission, begging, generosity, coercion, etc. can be readily recognized cross-culturally. However, each culture has its own peccadilloes when it comes to the expressions of status: gestures, ornaments, possessions, postures, rituals, even languages themselves. As Leary writes, "At one point a Cadillac car indicates highest status; shortly later a Cadillac indicates a pimp or cocaine dealer from the slums. And so it goes." Second circuit dynamics involve group communication and cooperation, whether it be between members of an insect colony, a primate troop, a beaver colony, human groups—herd-like behavior, from which intricate social networks can emerge. An individual's survival depends upon sensitivity to social differences—where one lies in the pecking order, or social web. In all group behavior the individual sacrifices some autonomy, and in many species the social dynamic is so extreme that no individual freedom is left at all. We have, sometimes sharp, division of emotional roles. The second circuit imprint determines emotional style and interpersonal ego. Wounding of pride can occur only when emotion is present.

The Pecking Order

Our mammalian territorial brains enable us to survive because they create the real, the symbolic and the moral home-turf we inhabit. Without this mediating function, we would be helpless organisms in the ecosystem and in society. The emotional intelligence designed to acknowledge and assert territorial claims, maintain individual autonomy and balance it within social power-dynamics, and adjust behavior appropriately to fulfill these needs, is what constitutes what we normally call *ego*. This is our functional concept of Earthbound self.

This stage of evolution deals with external manifestations of emotions in social structures—a.k.a. the pecking order. Our second brains can regulate endocrine and motor systems to enable us to maintain just the right level of dominance-submission.

Defenders of Turf

Many people who take a heavy imprint on the second circuit tend to be very athletic or muscular types, having concentrated their energy in their attack/defend functions and being somewhat, or quite, pugnacious. Not all but most military recruits fall into this category, and it is fitting that they become involved in the overarching "defense" of our tribal turf, which has of course by now become rather abstract, given the paucity of military threats. As RAW notes, military speech is heavily influenced by the anal orientation of this circuit: "ass" means one's entire self, and "shit" refers to all of the circumstances surrounding it.

Ego-Self

The functions of this circuit are associated with the hypothalamus, located at the mid-brain. This neural circuit commands ATP muscular-adrenaline and endocrine systems to foster attack, retreat, evasion, dominance, all in the name of control. As Leary said, we are all, to some extent, moody ego-dictators. For example, children throw temper tantrums in order to gain attention, status and some measure of control over a situation. Does this remind you of any politicians?

The alpha male syndrome in ethology embodies the emotional-territorial stage. Along these lines, children are brought up to believe that one is the master of one's fate, that one can make a difference in the world, that one is captain over one's own soul—this all stems from the dominant understanding of ego in society. The hero of all popular movies, books, TV shows, comics, etc. is always powerful and in control, but I think (or I hope) most adults realize that this is pure fantasy.

The emotional-territorial circuit is, interestingly, what we are talking about when we use the word *ego*. The ego is the organism's neurological construct for negotiating territorial group dynamics in human societies, or in wolf-packs, or in flocks, etc. It is our standard sense of self when we are not really paying attention, and sometimes things get a little confusing. "Ego" is essentially the program that deals with one's interplay with the pack—one's status. It is *a* self, not necessarily *the* self. As Lieutenant Commander Spock reminds us, "Insults are effective only when emotion is present." Without an emotional circuit, there would be no ego to get bruised.

This is the realm of the social mammal or bird, with herds, packs, troops, flocks, pecking order. One engages in survival not merely through strength but also social communication—gestural, not symbolic.

The bureaucracies of Nazi Germany, Soviet Russia, the Inquisition and the Roman empire were all webs of relationships built around second circuit drives. Much of our own modern legal and political system, wherever property rights are concerned, works in much the same way, at bottom.

Emotional Language

The sophistication of the first and second circuits is roughly comparable among all mammals. I have observed, for example, that dogs are every bit as emotional as any human I have ever known. Real differences only begin to emerge when we introduce the third circuit, and even this is quite muddy because many animals, such as elephants, many primate species, dolphins and whales, and others, have demonstrated, in some cases extensive, third circuit proficiency. As a general rule we ought to tone down the anthropocentrism and realize that we are much more the same as our animal cousins than we are different. The present work asserts that the third, fourth and higher circuits may not necessarily be exclusively the domain of *homo sapiens*, and that the picture may be even more complex than we have previously thought. It is my experience that dogs, for example, understand people very well, in ways that some of their human counterparts do not, by tuning into cues on the first and second circuits (and even the third and fourth, when they are broadcasting the former's signals). Body language and vocal cadence are the primary ways dogs interpret what humans are thinking, and this interchange is very real for them, whereas to us it is quite unconscious. Humans express both safety and danger signals, and every form of emotion, in ways that are quite understandable to canines, but often not even noticed by other humans. It has even been suggested that dogs are better judges of character than people, and this is not an unreasonable statement, given the fact that humans are wrapped up in subjective language and do not notice very many of the other signals which are being broadcast—ones that are not filtered by a human agenda. I feel that canines know us much better than we realize, and this stands to reason, as we share a significant portion of our circuitry with them, and we have been around each other for so long. We would do very well to get out of the millennia-old rut that has it that humans are fundamentally different than animals. As the present work hopes to show, such a notion is foolish.

CIRCUIT 3

The Rational-Mental-Symbolic

The third circuit, which involves dexterity, symbolism, reasoning, semantics, generational time binding—the "mind"—makes a "map," or "model," or "reality-tunnel," which can be passed on to others, from both the living and the dead. Third circuit signals can spread across many generations. This is why a poor, itinerant fisherman from rural, Roman Palestine can have such a noteworthy effect even two thousand years after his death—his message is encoded in many symbols, in many symbol systems, which are available to very many people. The maps of which I speak take many forms: the spoken or written word, in the form of poetry or prose; music; art; scientific theories; tools; concepts; artifacts of all sorts. The third circuit contains universes of information, most of which we take for granted and do not even notice, as we are immersed in its function unconsciously, much as a trout in a babbling brook has no real cognizance of water. In much the same way, we are not aware of the hidden biases and cultural colorings of the languages we speak, and even these languages are transmitting signals through time that, though hidden, have fantastically consequential effects on the events of history. The third circuit is a system, and you're in it, and you couldn't get out if you wanted to. But there is, indeed, much to enjoy, and you absolutely could not function in human society without it.

Everything you learned in school, and in Sunday school, consisted of third circuit symbols transmitted across space and time through symbol systems. Perhaps what makes humans unique, or at least unusual, in the animal kingdom, is our *self-reflective, symbolic thought*. This is how human language, and human culture, are made possible. Everything you know of Lao-Tzu, Buddha, Jesus, Muhammad, not to mention Alexander the Great, Genghis Khan, Julius Caesar, Napoleon; and Copernicus, Galileo, Newton, Einstein, Socrates, Plato, Shakespeare and Beethoven, is nothing more or less than the transmission of symbols, passed from one generation to the next in an unbroken chain. Both the knowledge of their existence, and the content of their message, is encoded in minute phonemes, often represented by symbols and combinations of symbols, denoting units of speech, which are built into words and sentences, with agreed upon meanings, to form a cultural system.

That humans can amass knowledge in this way is nothing short of extraordinary, and we are all made up of all sorts of signals, probably hundreds of thousands of them, that make us who we are, tell us what we know, and enable us to communicate to others all this and more. We do not rule symbols; symbols rule us. Remember that. The inventors of the wheel and the alphabet, the Roman empire—its roads, engineering and language; explorers, conquistadores, grain merchants, water managers, Greek philosophers, medieval kings, Constantine the Great: all of these ideas make us who we are, literally, and when you stop and think about it, they are all nothing but combinations of symbols, or phonemes (even more fundamentally). We've never seen, touched, heard or smelled any of these people or things, yet we are here in part because of all of them, and our knowledge about them is quite extensive. That is the power of symbols, and that is the reality of the third circuit.

Time-Binding and Cultural Evolution

The bio-survival circuit divides experience into two factors: that which is safe and nourishing, and that which is dangerous or threatening. Likewise, the emotional-territorial circuit divides experience into that which is more powerful, or has a greater claim to a given territory (and territory has multiple connotations here), and that which is less powerful, or has a lesser claim to a given territory—lower in the "pecking order." The rational-mental circuit is different. It allows us to subdivide, classify, and arrange our conceptual models at will. There is a dichotomy in the sense of the dialectic—we tend to place our thinking in polarities. But aside from this essential duality, we can make whatever connections we wish, and be right or wrong to our heart's content. The concomitant development of culture occurs through the generational time-binding dimension, in which adjustments and refinements are made in essentially the way we see technology develop.

It would be a mistake to say that this is all done consciously, or according to some plan, as so many factors are involved, and there is such an element of chance and random connection. But our symbol-systems are like a doorway through time, and as people down through the ages make their mark on previous history, and their descendants make their mark on theirs, we have the phenomena of cultural evolution, technological development, and history. As the mental-rational circuit's maps grow through this generational time-binding process, new maps and new technologies enter the picture at more and more rapid rates. It is interesting to note that a hundred years ago, many people were still travelling by horse-and-buggy. Since then we have had the microwave, the space shuttle and the internet. It seems quite clear that development is "speeding up." That is, the information content and technical capacity of human knowledge are increasing exponentially as time goes on. Much more happens in a decade now than did fifty years ago. And in twenty years' time, more will happen in one year than now happens in five. There are huge ramifications to all of this, and the process encompasses more than just third circuit time-binding, but such time-binding is the crucial avenue that makes it all possible.

Games and Sanity

The highly civilized human can master hundreds of laryngeal-manual symbol systems. An educated individual of the twenty-first century can speak and write in several languages, manipulate a wide variety of mechanical artifacts, professional techniques, mathematical and scientific formulae, sports and games. And the progression toward greater complexity seems to be getting faster and faster all the time.

Imprinted and conditioned by human symbol systems, this circuit deals primarily with artifacts and language. This circuit classifies everything in the environment according to the culture in which one is immersed—the local reality-tunnel. The symbolic thought of this circuit leads to creativity, invention, calculation and prediction (science) and the transmission of the signals arising from these functions across generations—via the spoken and written word.

A child growing up finds stability and consistency in the sociocultural cues she imprints. Her parents and neighbors speak the same language and share rituals and behaviors with those in the group with which she comes to identify. This "consensus" reality provides the illusion of a rigid, objective universe with certain characteristics which is shared by the entire cultural group. "Sanity" is defined in terms of one's ability to adhere as closely as possible to the established story of how things are and how things came to be a certain way within a particular society. A purportedly sane Blackfoot would tell you that the Old Man of the Sun created the Earth just as an ancient Greek would say the dark, silent abyss of Chaos gave birth to Gaia, which brought forth Ouranos, etc. Any public deviation from such established beliefs would have been at odds with society, and any deviation that was substantial enough might engender an assertion that its proponent was no longer sane. The perception that one is perceiving what others are is paramount in any society. And consequently, it has been shown by countless researchers that humans naturally and easily distort objective actuality to fit psychological expectations.

Subjective Reason

Carl Jung gave a particularly elegant breakdown of the first three circuits. He stipulated that the first circuit mediates *sensation*, the second circuit *feeling*, and the third circuit *reason*. It is important to realize that no one circuit operates in a vacuum, however. All three affect each of the other three, and there are feedbacks, filters and resonances in complex interplays among all of the circuits. Someone can give an "emotional speech." Politicians, indeed, play to their bases by charging language and sloganeering with emotion, and even with signaling there is tribal safety and security to be found if they are victorious. The very notion of nationalism is also a combination of all three circuits—we have our anthems and our pledges, which exist as time-bound, symbolic language which is designed to play on the concept of our property being more sacred than anyone else's, because we are the strongest and the most "free." In this way we can see that "reason" is quite vulnerable to manipulation by the lower, less sophisticated circuits, and that many ideas paraded about under the guise of being "reasonable" are really nothing more than emotionally-charged power-plays or prejudices, including racism, bigotry, xenophobia, patriotism, fanaticism and all sorts of intolerant ideologies. Even though these ideas are communicated at a third circuit level, they are really centered on nothing more than base emotion, fear and insecurity. Remember—we are primates. And as Luther famously said, "Reason is a whore."

Most people, as we all know, are quite stubborn in their views, and are more often than not very difficult to convince of any sort of idea that does not match their rigid, already formed beliefs. Using third circuit signals to try to persuade them of certain notions usually fails, however reasonable or well-intentioned these notions may seem or in fact be. This is, once again, a confluence of the first and second circuits perverting the judgment of the third. When a set of ideas—and we see this all the time in election years—does not line up with preconceived notions, even though they may be in a given person's very best interest, there is very likely not going to be any reasonable thinking going on at all. The new or different suggestions more often than not threaten a person at the level of his or her second circuit. In an abstract but very real way, a person is deathly afraid of loss of status. If a Republican were asked to adopt Democratic views, this would be regarded as a threat to status, as the Republican in question identifies with the party, and feels a sense of belonging that would be threatened by becoming something of a turncoat. More than that, people are usually quite proud of the picture of the world that has been formed in their heads, and any suggestion of change to this edifice would be a challenge to the ideological "space" or headspace of someone who is asked to think differently. Such a notion of mental space may seem abstract, but it is perfectly real; first and second circuit functions often have ideational superstructures in the mind, which are usually not terribly rational but merely a veil for emotion. Unfortunately, we live in a world, not where reason dominates, but where emotion does.

Abstracted Space

On the first circuit, we have the configuration of advance/retreat—we move toward what is safe or beneficial, and we retreat from what is dangerous or engenders uncertainty. On the second circuit, we have the configuration of up and down, or top/bottom—we exist in a pecking order, in which those with the most power are at the top, and those with the least at the bottom. The third circuit brings another dimension into play: left and right. We are oriented, in our manipulation of artifacts, to use our hands. This creates a real dimension in which, in a significant way, we divide the world into left and right. Written language also contains this dimension in some cultures, as most in the world read and write in either a left to right or right to left fashion. (There are of course some cultures which utilize vertical writing systems, but they are in the global minority, and most of these employ horizontal writing as well). So we have, therefore, forward/back, up/down, and left/right—an orientation that gives rise to Euclidean space as we know it. It is no coincidence that geometry and later physics created a theoretical foundation based upon Euclidean space, as, intuitively, this is the set of dimensions that is most natural to us. Subsequent developments in mathematics and physics have proven that this system is only correct in a limited range, and that fundamentally, the dimensionality of the universe is quite a bit more complex, in truth. Euclidean space, then, is largely a kind of projection humans make based upon the bio-survival, emotional, and mental circuits. This is how space is defined for us.

Live Long and Prosper

Many individuals who take their heaviest imprint on the third circuit become intensely distrustful and even hostile toward first and second circuit functions. The playfulness with the environment that is a key first circuit behavior, as well as the whole range of human emotions, can be baffling, confusing, frightening and embarrassing to most mental-rational types. We may here think of that most charming Vulcan, Commander Spock, who embodied these notions. Human emotion, romance and biased reasoning were all irrational and to be avoided at all costs by this wonderful character on *Star Trek*. As I have pointed out, that show was a stellar exemplar of the very model about which this book attempts to communicate. If you look carefully at any episode, or any of the films, you can see every circuit, from 1-8, represented in some fashion. Try to see it that way next time you watch it!

Restrictive Imprints

The semantic circuit, just like circuits one and two, is essentially restricted by whatever imprint is has happened to take. All conditioning and learning are built upon this imprint, and are therefore restricted to what is allowed by it; in the majority of people, a socially acceptable, and therefore somewhat predictable, imprint has usually been formed. All members of a given culture, and especially those who are bound by a common language, with common idiosyncrasies, will generally have a similar range of 1. what is acceptable to think privately and 2. what is acceptable to communicate to others. It is for this reason that observed behaviors are usually coincident with expected behaviors. Now, there is a virtual infinity of existentially thinkable thoughts. But many, perhaps most, of these possible thoughts are socially and culturally unthinkable. The parameters of the cultural sphere (about which more will be discussed regarding circuit four) affect what we are allowed to think, say and do, but moreover, restrict the form most imprints are likely to take, creating perhaps some feedback mechanism, and a way for culture to regulate itself—in an abstract sense.

There are those who escape this, potentially by having circuit seven insights, thereby creating novel and sometimes radical third circuit maps that no one had thought of before. We often refer to such types with the label "genius." Needless to say, most of the time these new models of experience that are introduced by such people are often met with misunderstanding and hostility, and can be shocking to those who are trapped in the robotic imprints that so define such a large portion of the population. As we have discussed, such a phenomenon can be a considerable threat to the established mental and ideological territory of people, and second circuit disapproval, or worse, is very often the result.

Even one of the smartest classes among us—the scientists—are not immune to this phenomenon. It took a generation, and the infusion of youth, before scientists willingly adopted Einstein's relativity, and the same can be said for quantum mechanics. The old guard of physics regarded it as nonsensically random, but after some years passed, young, up-and-coming students took it up without a second thought—because it explained experiment precisely! The older denizens of the scientific community were so mechanically hooked into their old imprints that they simply would not accept the revolutionary new theories, which they regarded as ridiculous. The only solution was to wait a generation for the neophobia to subside. This has happened repeatedly throughout the history of science. As rational as they are, I suppose it helps to remember that such minds are as human as the rest of us, indeed. And as RAW pointed out, if science has roughly a generation-length time-lag, what of politics, philosophy, economics, etc.?

Time

The experience of time is a noteworthy feature on each of the first three circuits. As previously mentioned, on the bio-survival circuit, there is no time at all. We react, and just find ourselves doing certain things. On the emotional-territorial circuit, time becomes a factor. We need time to assess a situation and "size-up" another who may have crossed over into our turf. Humans also often agonize about emotional decisions, and time is a key factor in the tension and suspense employed by many writers and filmmakers. On the third circuit, time becomes fully experienced, but in addition to this perceived dimension, we *conceptualize* time here as well. All of our stories, from the Bible to Shakespeare, come to us from luminary figures of the distant past. Our use of language, especially written language, creates the time-binding that enables us to span millennia with our signals. Science introduces mammoth time-scales that boggle the mind, but that are fundamental to the workings of nature. It is hard to relate to a nanosecond, and even harder to relate to thirteen billion years! But humans have indeed mapped these territories. Time becomes perhaps even more of a factor on the fourth circuit, giving extra meaning and value to what time we have. Not to jump ahead too much, but the nature of time becomes ever deeper as we ascend to the higher circuits. More on that later!

CIRCUIT 4

The Social and Sexual

Circuit four involves moral and social values, and is involved in the system of neurotransmitters linked with sexuality, friendship, and all social activity. At this level, there are many variations across cultures, as what is considered moral in one society may be taboo or unthinkable in another. For example, in the more conservative Muslim countries, women may not show their faces or any patch of skin whatsoever; in the secular West, where dressing liberally is now the norm for many women, we see this as fundamentalist nonsense. (Perhaps the conservatism of some Muslims in dress has a rational and positive meaning, at least for them, but I digress). The basic sperm-egg invitations to sexual congress are of course the same the world over, but the pertinent language, values, inhibitions, expressions, sublimations, etc. of socio-sexual behavior vary dramatically across the globe.

The majority of humans live in tremendous fear of being seen as sinful or "bad." What is socially approved and acceptable is very much on the minds of most people, most of the time.

As exemplars of socio-sexual morality, we have people like Muhammad, who was a polygamist, and Luther, who was a paternalist, both producing moral systems of the same bent—prudish, exploitative, chauvinistic at times, and paternalistic. We see associated social responsibilities determining the norms for virtue and sin—which are, ultimately, always sexual in origin. This is the true nature of proximate human morality.

The circuit is imprinted by early orgasm-mating experiences at puberty and conditioned by local tribal mores and taboos. It processes sexual pleasure; social interactions such as relationships and even friendship; local definitions of "right" and "wrong"; most functions associated with reproduction; the adult-parental awareness, personality and sex role; and ensures the nurture of the young. The sensation of "love" (via the oxytocin neurotransmitter) is central to all of this.

The Fourth Circuit defines socio-sexual roles which may differ as much as the caste types in an insect colony. A large percentage of humans are not designed for procreation and parenthood, but are wired to play other useful and meaningful domesticated roles.

Chaotic Imprints

The socio-sexual circuit is activated and imprinted at puberty, when the DNA-robot achieves the level of maturity for this apparatus to be hormonally instructed to fully awaken. The adolescent teenager enters the rut, and begins not only to notice but to go a little crazy about the opposite sex. Of course the whole purpose of all of this, and really that of all Earthly life, is to encourage sperm-egg fusion as a means for DNA to do what it does: replicate and continue its journey. This frenzy over mating has sustained our species for over 100,000 years on the one hand, and led to a planetary population of 8 billion and climbing on the other. I leave it to the reader to decide whether this is a healthy level for the planet, or our species, but the relentless sort of logic of the fourth circuit is clearly effective, in terms of evolutionary strategy.

Imprint vulnerability is every bit as sensitive for this circuit as the others, and the imprint every bit as reliant on fortune, as this concretization remains fixed for life, forever defining the individual's sexual identity and reality, for good or ill. The observable range of sexual fetishes and behaviors is therefore unsurprising in its scope, given the randomness and extensive possibility involved in just what might happen at that moment of imprinting. Would that nature weren't so cruel to so many! It's not always cruel, though, as we all know. Characteristics like homosexuality or heterosexuality, promiscuity or chastity, philandering or celibacy, bizarre fetishes, etc., all arise for the most part from that imprinting stimulus, and are, the vast majority of the time, with us for life.

Domesticity

Any parent can relate to the fact that when conception and, later, birth of the baby occur, dramatic biochemical changes appear in both the mother and father. This is a function of one's fourth circuit kicking into gear to make for loved and protected offspring, as the responsible mom and dad become motivated in their new role as overseers of the domestic household. These are, despite the tacit assumptions of most, completely robotic behaviors. Evolution takes no chances in the protection and propagation of its seed. It is very important that the parents feel they are sacrificing themselves for the good of the children. This is a very old bio-program. Without it, none of us would be here.

The domesticated household and the socio-sexual circuitry go hand-in-hand. There is a clear pattern in the young in which, after an adolescence and young-adulthood of idealism, rebelliousness, wildness, independence, there is a metamorphosis to an adult prudence, practicality, docility and productivity whereby the individual can make a steady living and become able to provide for a family. There are of course very many who do not find themselves in such a domestic role, but for the purposes of propagating DNA, this is the essence of the game. This change usually occurs due to hormonal, biochemical signals, as it is a robot behavior and, as previously stated, the evolutionary process could not have gotten on without it. For most, the parental brain is activated in this way. It goes without saying, however, that not all men or women are "selected" for parental roles by their DNA. There are a wide range of socio-sexual realities. Indeed, society has no problem with non-parental roles as long as they are perceived to be contributing to the common good. The Pope, and all manner of assorted clergy throughout the world's religions, give prime examples. There have been many bachelor politicians, astronauts. Homosexuals of all stripes would be included. In a kind of group selection, if you have something to offer, you need not necessarily embody the ubiquitous nuclear family archetype. But then, socio-sexuality is clearly complex.

Group Morality

Aboriginal peoples are well-known for their rituals surrounding the entrance to manhood for males, and the first menses for females, and these rituals are no more or less than cultural devices for controlling, or at least ordering as much as possible, the socio-sexual imprinting process of their young. These rituals involve ordeals, such as, for men, long treks into the wild with no tools or food provided, or the isolation of females from all of the men of the tribe while they endure a purification ritual that is often rather brutal. All of this is designed to imprint the desired traits of a proper member of the tribe, and for the most part the anthropological record shows that it was an effective way to preserve the integrity and the continued success of those tribes who engaged in such rituals. We really have nothing so orderly today, relying instead on anachronistic past relics of the aforementioned rituals, such as baptism, confirmation, bar mitzvahs, marriage ceremonies, etc. As to our imprints, we now rely exclusively on accidents—chance, genetic factors, traumatic episodes, anger, fear, luck, etc. that create the imprints at the point of vulnerability. This leaves many people okay, some great, and others terrible. But that is the nature of it. Because of this, hardly anyone imprints the officially (culturally) sanctioned socio-sexual role of their society. Instead, most people have something to hide, and only *mimic* the accepted sex role for their gender, in their tribe. Perhaps there is no such thing as 'normal' here.

Every culture, every tribe, implicitly stipulates that the sexual behaviors must be regulated and enforced by that tribe. There has been no people in the history of the world that violated this principle; there must be rules for socio-sexual behavior, and to fail to abide by them means ostracism or worse. Aside from this, no other taboo is universal. This one is. There is a trap here, and it is known as relativism, but when one considers the fact that these cultural mores are *proximate*, not *ultimate*—that they are evolutionary, and pertain to the tribe's cultural evolution and not necessarily to any known truth—the confusion can be resolved. The system by which the phenomena of sexual attraction, mating, reproduction and genetic inheritance are regulated is known, indeed, as *morality*. Taboo and morality are evolutionary attempts to govern the random element in this complex sexual universe, and to select or create, as much as possible, a desired future cultural outcome.

A Moral Imperative

One example of a moral imperative is the encouragement to have as many offspring as possible in Mormon families. Of course, in a sociocultural sense, this has a perfectly pragmatic function, going all the way back to Joseph Smith and Brigham Young. The idea is to generate as large a population as possible, in order both to spread the religion and inflate its ranks as much as can be done, to create a larger working class in order to generate robust and successful business. Utah is, after all, known as the "beehive state." This was crucial both for the granting of statehood to the Mormons, and their success as a tribe thereafter. Catholicism used to preach similar tactics. To a Mormon or an old-school Catholic, such behaviors were construed to be commanded by the biblical directive to 'multiply and replenish,' in order to better subjugate the planet and make room for God's children. Moreover, a large family was considered good in itself, as the love shared is considered more sacred with more children and siblings. The real reason for it, however, was the one I outlined; church leaders had very real problems to solve, and by setting up such an ideological imperative, everyone was satisfied in their own way. Thus we see a moral system governing the microcosm and the macrocosm, to everyone's mutual benefit.

Sin

The idea of sin arises from the fact that no one has a perfectly matching cultural imprint on the fourth circuit; everyone diverges from the "norm" at least a little, and in many cases a lot, and certain institutions, mainly organized religion, have historically exerted themselves, in many cases primarily, toward the business of forgiveness of sins and atonement. For good or ill, this age-old function is being rather quickly dissolved in the modern age, and now morality seems to be enforced strictly based upon culturally sanctioned behavior, regulated by nothing other than social convention. But because the fourth circuit is real and singular, this is being done even without religion. Secular morality now rules, and while it is more flexible than during the times of ubiquitous conservative dogma, there is still an awful lot of shame generated. We are not, even still, especially enlightened socio-sexually.

Fourth Circuit Attachment

The primary function of the fourth circuit is, as we have discussed, to propagate the genes, and this is done through creating an "adult personality" that is responsible for and chiefly concerned with care for the young, most especially one's own. The primary evolutionary role of the fourth circuit is parenting. It is unsurprising that this circuit not only enables us to care *for* our offspring, but to care very much *about* them, to which any parent can relate. Love for one's children is considered by many to be the greatest good, and though it is a completely robotic behavior—one does not choose to love, it simply happens mechanically—perhaps this does not invalidate its sublimity. It is interesting to note that this circuit is discussed in the Eastern religions as the one that causes the most attachment—that binds one the most rigidly to the wheel of *samsara*. Mystics are famous for their renunciation of the attachment caused by this circuit, being known for their independent monasticism and shunning of the "lower" circuits entirely. In the Eastern monasteries, this fourth circuit attachment is ritualistically decimated by the infamous vow of celibacy. Some may cringe at this, and fail to understand it, but it is undoubtedly effective, and opens the path to liberation for many a committed pupil. Some people may wish to hold onto their attachment; others may boldly reject it. Either way, one hopes compassion survives.

Who Loves not Love?

The fourth circuit is linked neurologically with the genitalia and the breasts. Its primary neurotransmitter, involved in social bonding, sexual reproduction, and child-rearing, is oxytocin. Sex, hugging, cuddling and protection all cause releases of this neurotransmitter. People who take their heaviest imprint on this circuit are more often than not quite good looking, or in other words, sexually attractive, advertising to the opposite sex that this is a healthy, fecund specimen conducive to rearing robust offspring. Of course, when we see beauty in another, what is really happening is that we are receiving high quality, high frequency mating signals. This is all, of course, a sound evolutionary strategy, and one can easily see how well it all works. Friendship is also a characteristic behavior induced by this circuit. A friend is someone for whom we have warm feelings, although not to the point of neurotransmitter intensity that we wish to have sex with them. Just because our feelings for a friend may not be that intense, however, does not diminish the meaning of friendship and indeed, many people secretly prefer their friends to their lovers all the time. The socio-sexual circuit is the glue that binds people together, as it has been going all the way back to our origins. And as Aleister Crowley remarked, "Who loves not love?"

Co-Evolution of Circuits

A major auxiliary function of the fourth circuit is to put a brake on the dialectical constructiveness of the third circuit. In other words, new, innovative and provocative ideas are very often considered immoral. Whether or not true "progress" is occurring in civilization, and it is not my intention to explore that here, morality is often at odds with the linear type of development that the third circuit naturally brings into being. An extreme version of this phenomenon can be found among the Amish, whose moral system rejects all but the most rudimentary forms of technology. If one thinks of the tendency as a spectrum, the Amish would be at one extreme, while most other cultures hover around the middle. There seems to be no culture in the world that is completely open to novelty for its own sake, but some countries are clearly more liberal than others.

Another example of a brake on progressive ideas would be the push for gay rights in the United States. Even twenty or thirty years ago, any suggestion of equal marriage rights for homosexuals would have been considered crazy, but now it is a very real issue, with millions of supporters. The moralists, usually quite religious, on the right side of the spectrum feel being gay is a choice and a sin, and are incensed at the notion of equal rights for anyone who would so flagrantly violate their notions of right and wrong. As third circuit ideologies and technologies evolve, there is a co-evolution with acceptable moral norms. These two forces push on one another, but since the Renaissance, there has been a clear path for third circuit ideas to complexify, and this has enabled us to go from horse-drawn carriages to the Space Shuttle in one person's lifetime. This is not to make any comment about progress itself, and there is still considerable pushback on certain facets of cultural evolution from moral forces within modern culture. Genetic engineering comes foremost to mind. The horror of many about "playing God" is very real, and some areas of biology are heavily encumbered in a way, because society is not yet ready for a revolution in this area. This is a perfect example of the "braking" function of the fourth circuit on the third. Whether we will ever be free from these sorts of dogma is a very difficult question to answer. One likes to think that as time goes on, humanity becomes wiser. I'm not sure there's too much evidence to support such a claim, though.

Waking Up

Robert Anton Wilson made the following statement: "Very simply, a totally aware, alert, *awakened* (unbrainwashed) person would not fit very well into any of the standard roles society offers; the damaged, robotized products of traditional child-rearing *do* fit into those slots." In other words, we have two breeds of cat in society. Those who are willingly locked into the social roles expected of them, and those who are not—who reject the established social order. This goes hand-in-hand with the phenomena we will be exploring in the next sections of the book—especially the sections detailing the "higher" circuits of the nervous system. Those souls who have at least some awareness of circuit 5—and higher—are generally not too keen about the nature of the establishment now dominant in most nations of the world. And that establishment is, let's face it, not too keen on them, either. This all played out during the 1960s, of course, and while revolution is not currently at the door, that basic configuration still exists—it's just that those making up the counterculture, for lack of a better word, are much less vociferous these days, and they don't really have a choice in that. Let us turn now to a general exploration, which will be followed by the higher strata of body and mind...

EXPLORATION

Conceptualizing Truth

The first four (evolutionary) circuits limit consciousness to imprint and conditioning programs, and give centrality to what is physically, emotionally, mentally and socially rewarding. This wiring is trained to perform goal-oriented, game-specific and essentially robotic sequences in a classical (Newtonian) framework. The billions of signals which course through the nervous system every minute—known to yogis, shamans and psychonauts—are, at this level, censored from awareness, as they would obstruct and confuse the normal survival functions of the organism. Thus, the four-brained individual is basically confined to robotic, reflex-wiring and cannot consciously control or meaningfully affect its own equipment.

Each nervous system is its own reality island. Truth is defined in relation to the wiring of the individual nervous system in question—the genetic, imprinted and conditioned reality. In fact, the human brain processes several billion signals every minute— multifaceted, tremendously varied—and these are mediated by the eight circuit system. Whatever interpretations the individual's imprinted, conditioned and learned symbol systems project onto these energies is defined as "true."

The task of disseminating and popularizing new and "mystical" philosophic themes has been assigned to those in special castes—artists, writers, poets, bards, minstrels, filmmakers, musicians, troubadours—storytellers of all kinds. For example, the Impressionists, Expressionists, Cubists, Pointillists, Surrealists and others created a gestalt-shift, or paradigm-shift of a sort, initiating the public into the heightened non-classical and relativistic space around the turn of the twentieth century that paralleled developments in physics at the time. If culture is to have meaning and relevance, this is a crucial function.

Imprints

Skinnerian operant conditioning occurs by means of immediate and continual reinforcement. Imprinting requires no reinforcement whatsoever. An imprinted schema is more or less set in stone, until such time as a biochemical shock serves to re-imprint the circuit. Once an infant is imprinted, no amount of conditioning during adolescence will change it. Once adolescent imprinting takes place, no amount of conditioning of the adult will reverse it. The imprint requires no repeated reward or punishment to be maintained, and is permanent. Conditioned associations, on the other hand, wane and disappear easily with lack of repetition. Moreover, neural imprints are by nature accidental. There are underground methods for performing or engineering a re-imprinting process, but no scientific method has yet been developed. Unfortunately, the prohibition of research on psychedelic substances has set development in this area back by about fifty years, and continues to halt most of the initiative of researchers who might otherwise develop studies along such lines.

No amount of conditioning will fundamentally change behavior. Skinnerian, behaviorist conditioning will fail as soon as reward-punishment controls are eased, which always results in a natural and inevitable return to the magnetism of the imprint.

Most domesticated citizens of the middle and working classes have imprinted docility and fear onto the template of their second circuit; repetitious symbol- or artifact-manipulation onto the third circuit; and shame onto the fourth circuit. Society's schools imprint children to be stupid so that it is a simple matter to quell any potential questioning of the status quo.

The inefficiency and ineffectiveness of psychological conditioning and the concreteness of imprints is seen most clearly in the fourth circuit. When was the last time a homosexual was "cured" of his orientation? Or sexual fetishes effectively erased? Imprinted lust stimuli are not an easy thing to alter. Once biochemical engravings are made in the neural circuitry, it is very difficult to erase them.

The DNA Robot

For practical purposes, the human organism exists in a consensus reality of the four basic evolutionary imprints. Although the brain is inundated with millions of signals each second, mundane consciousness is limited to signals corresponding to one of these four imprints at any given time. In other words, reality is filtered through neural programs in such a way as to leave only allowed perceptions into awareness; in point of fact, there are many coherent thought-constructs that get left out. Most people, unless one is communicating on a level meaningful for them (circuits 1-4), will ignore, misunderstand, or become hostile if challenged with signals that for them are unusual and incomprehensible. Typically, permissible behaviors are ones that offer benefit or threat on the four basic levels: bio-survival safety and well-being; emotional-hierarchical status; artifact manipulation, especially via acceptable language; and social-sexual security within the hive status quo. Most common interactions occur very much along these four survival lines. The majority of humans now living, and long dead, have communicated in mostly rote fashion along these four channels, scanning automatically for the pertinent survival signals from another and reacting like robots, mechanically moving from place to place and task to task only experiencing a very tiny sliver of reality, while fearful of and hostile to anything that does not exist inside of it.

Communication occurs on the aforementioned four evolutionary levels, some of which is comprehensible to the entire species generally, and some of which can only be understood by members of the same culture (which is composed of similar in-group imprints). Most individuals are not comfortable with the information they receive unless it fits into their third circuit tunnel-reality (or map), and also jibes with their second circuit emotional status. The candidacy of Donald Trump made a lot of sense to some, and seemed ridiculous to many others, for example.

New symbols are typically learned only when there is a special motivation to do so, and usually this is built upon established emotional and mental systems, when there is the promise of some direct future reward or benefit. Such a situation is rather exceptional in modern society, and so we see dominant ideologies perpetuated endlessly. Most people resist adamantly learning new symbols which may challenge or even modify their existing mental and emotional frameworks. This resistance is not psychological, but rather neurological and thus bio-chemical. It is virtually impossible, most of the time, for people to undertake a change that would require a literal re-wiring of their own nervous systems; therefore, we rarely see significant transformations.

Communicating with the majority involves working inside their network of channels. Each idea presented must resonate with the reality-tunnel already established, or meaningful communication cannot take place. Most people learn no new symbol systems after childhood, instead adding onto and working within symbols closely associated with the imprint. This may have quite a bit to do with the fact that it often takes at least one generation for a new idea or theory to be understood—a new paradigm is only ever really established after young, new minds pick up the new ideas and make them commonplace. It is important to remember, in communicating with the majority, that there are very few symbols established to deal with the higher circuits; therefore, overzealousness is to be avoided by the judicious.

It is nearly impossible to discuss meaningful philosophy with yokels. It is nearly impossible to translate the vicissitudes of awareness on the higher circuits with people who have never experienced them (and probably never will). Sexual and ethical matters are likewise anathema to the closed-minded. As Leary pointed out, hypocrisy, unconscious motivation, irrational paradox, the need for approval, and fear of shame tend to dominate the thoughts of the masses.

Most humans may tune out certain circuit 3 symbols when they are bored or challenged by them, or if they do not fit with their imprints or conditioned networks. But circuit 4 signals and behaviors which are sensed as different are more often than not met with either passive or active hostility, which can create a passionate response and in some cases even violence. This philosophical sensitivity is one reason why yokel humans instinctively avoid philosophical matters.

We are all DNA-robots. Most of us blindly labor in order to breed, raise offspring, and perpetuate human society, which is primarily concerned with the facilitation of sex and the avoidance of death. All that we are has been "designed" to propagate DNA. Therefore, those of us who are most robotized are quite threatened when that robotism is pointed out and questioned. This is all quite scary, if it is even comprehensible, to the average human, thus such thinking is staunchly avoided by most.

Higher Circuits

The experience of higher circuits has been described in countless reports by poets, mystics, occultists, psychedelic adepts, and the like. In common language, these visionary reports have appeared vague and subjective, when they have not been considered delusional or psychotic, as they often are by people of all stripes. There are surely many ways to classify visionary experience, but perhaps the most basic and fundamental method is the stipulation of three higher circuits of neurological scope, plus one that is meta-neurological and meta-physiological. The neurological circuits are: neurosomatic intelligence, which pertains to the neurological circuitry for somatic-sensory signals; neurogenetic intelligence, which pertains to the transception of DNA signals within the neuron; and neuroelectric intelligence, or metaprogramming, which pertains to relativistic, multiple-choice brain awareness, or true will. The eighth circuit is beyond matter, energy, space and time completely. These circuits can be activated naturally, via advanced meditation or severe shocks, or artificially, by certain chemical neurotransmitters.

Modern psychology has not incorporated these levels of the nervous system largely through ignorance but also because of the stigma surrounding applicable research or even the willingness to accept that such thinking has any bearing on reality. Most Ph.D.s, while their expertise is appreciable, have not experienced these realities and therefore, like most scientists, do not even entertain their possibility. Therefore, such mental states are often labeled as meaningless hallucinations, dream-states, etc. when, as I have suggested above, they are not considered as the insanity produced in a disordered mind. These notions are reinforced by the fact that such expanded mental states are at odds with the normal, domesticated tunnel-reality of well-heeled members of society, so, doubtless, some people may feel threatened by or very uncomfortable with them, and this is really no fault of theirs.

The Sage

Neurosomatic and neuroelectric neurotransmitter chemicals have been used widely in the past by shamans, alchemists, yogis, and so forth, leading to varied and remarkable mystical, prophetic, otherworldly descriptions. The opponents of such neurotransmitter chemicals are legitimately fearful of such radical departures from consensus-reality, though their contention that these chemicals are irrelevant or extremely dangerous is perhaps rather ill-founded.

There are some modern individuals who display facility with higher circuit functions, though they are a minority, and there have been a few in every age. Psychics, mediums, prophets, gurus, mystics, philosophers, visionary artists, poets come to mind. One must also include idiot savants, and eccentric geniuses of all stripes, many of whom were forced into insane asylums for being a little too "far out." In fact, many indigenous tribes valued strongly the characteristics of psychosis that were exhibited by their shamans and medicine men, who were highly prized individuals for what were considered to be great spiritual gifts.

Such complex souls typically have no sanctioned place in modern society. They are unacknowledged, and invisible to the great majority. What Leary calls the "Cyber-Individual" is someone who has detached from the staid, stale, often toxic imprints widely held by the dominant global collective—someone who has cut ties from the family, the gene-pool, the governments and institutions of the world order. He or she has taken over responsibility and understanding of his or her own body, brain, DNA and neuro-atomic realities. Many sages are known to have done this sort of thing; perhaps it's no surprise we have so few sages!

Degrees of Order

Modern popular scientific thinking has it, with respect to the latest findings in physics, chemistry and biology, that all life, indeed all we see, is a "mad dance of atoms." Without going into how this is a veiled re-hash of classical, Cartesian "billiard-ball" thinking, it needs to be said that there is nothing random or accidental involved with such processes. As David Bohm pointed out, everything in the universe has a degree of order. A "mad dance of atoms" may or may not have a low degree of order—and it may indeed be chaotic—but it is never truly random.

The Judeo-Christian West seems to be stuck in a Newtonian/Cartesian rigidity, while the core of, for example, Chinese thought, particularly of Lao-Tzu, Buddha and Confucius, seems to be at a relatively primitive level of quasi-Einsteinian sophistication. They are personal, relativistic, highly logical doctrines which are very process-oriented, making them right-off-the-bat more accommodating of scientific theory than any of the traditions in the West. They avoid the Aristotelian tendency only to consider either-or opposites, and shun the notion of static, formulaic "truths."

Specialization

Each of us is genetically wired to have a preponderance of one circuit dominating all the others. This generally determines our adult specialization, and any sort of niche at any level of social existence we may inhabit. It is also what causes us to become rigid and lack flexibility as we age. Specializations by their very nature cause our growth to stop, our perspective to wither, and our plasticity to become concretized. Unfortunately, modern capitalist society is based upon the need for extreme specialization. Looking at this reality, I am very glad that I am a generalist. I would rather know some about a lot than everything about virtually nothing.

A Call for Compassion

If an improper first circuit imprint is made, some form of deep distrust, alienation, autism, or bio-survival schizophrenia can result. If an improper second circuit imprint is made, and regular mammalian reality is not imprinted, territorial-emotional schizophrenia may result, possibly involving emotional alienation, sociopathy, the loser-outlaw—a Lee Harvey Oswald type. If an improper mental, consensual-reality imprint is made, third circuit schizophrenia can ensue—mental insanity; cultural illiteracy; inability to think or reason in a constructive or collaborative way; bizarre, odd-ball personal philosophies; bigotries; fanatical sects of all sorts; paranoia. Fourth circuit schizophrenia can result in any of a variety of forms of pathological shame, and an inability to empathize and sympathize with other members of one's own or another tribe. It behooves us to remember that, with all of the blind chance involved in neurological imprinting (and genetics), and with all of the varieties of aberration that depart from the mean as a result of this, tolerance, compassion and kindness are probably a sound policy.

The Neurosomatic Type

As mentioned elsewhere, the major shift that was the sixties comprised a revolution in fifth circuit awareness among segments of the population, particularly the youth. A major theme was control of the body for individual pleasure, along with the use of neurosomatic and psychedelic substances, sexual freedom, freedom of dress and grooming, refusal to allow the government to use one's body as an instrument of violence (draft resistance) and refusal to permit the greater society to continue to use people as economic tools (a la the infamous "drop-out" philosophy). As a corollary, there was significant resistance to the practice (by many governments) of using fifth circuit sensory stimuli to coerce, recondition or torture. These all became political issues, either explicitly or implicitly, and served to define that decade.

Most fifth circuit adepts (and certainly those who have facility with circuits higher than that) are essentially invisible to the rest of society. They are not really playing the game, they are not interacting to a high degree with the lower-circuited majority, and they are fine with this—they're not interested in all of those meaningless games. They are generally law-abiding citizens (with the exception of using banned psychedelic chemicals to some degree), as they have no use for committing serious crimes. A world full of these types of people would be a radically different place, indeed.

The Psychological Reality

It has become clear that brain-mind functions are fabulously complex, perhaps much more so than was previously thought, and the problem of consciousness is, among neuroscientists and philosophers, as intractable as it ever was. It has even been suggested by some that the brain operates in dimensions higher than just the familiar 4-D reality to which we are accustomed, and that strange phenomena like synchronicity are the result of contact with a fundamental ground that is common to both the object and the subject of perception. The neurological circuits which we are discussing may be part of a multidimensional structure which has infinitely greater scope than the Earthly, primate reality in which we have evolved and been programmed to live. The potential exists that there is a wide spectrum of vibrations of which we are not normally aware, but which are available to the deeper layers of our subconscious—a rich tapestry of unrestricted and dazzlingly structured reality that is blocked by the survival functions of our nervous systems, which would strongly prefer that we focus on survival in the here and now. These phenomena transcend our narrow, myopic reality-tunnels, and have the potential to explode our rigid perceptions and staid conceptualizations of evolutionary reality—of our normal awareness of space and time.

Every set of neurological programs has four basic, underlying aspects: *Genetic Necessities*: Completely hard-wired programs, e.g. instincts (like those defined by Sociobiology); *Imprints*: More or less hard-wired programs which arise from programmable genetic constructs and which are set in place by environmental triggers during periods of "imprint vulnerability," in which certain behavioral patterns are formed by critical experiences; *Conditioning*: Less fundamental programs which are built onto the imprints and which are looser and much easier to change than imprints with counter-conditioning; *Learning*: Memory-based functions which are even softer than conditioning—they can be forgotten or modified much more easily than programs on the previous three levels, and do not determine behavior to the degree that the previous levels do. Imprints will most often overrule any subsequent conditioning or learning, and are, along with genetics, the primary determinants of almost all primate and animal behavior. An imprint starts out as a kind of software that is then immediately turned into built-in hardware, and can only be changed in very exceptional circumstances. Imprints form the basis of our personality and our individuality, and establish the set parameters in which all conditioning and learning may occur. These four levels constitute the primary psychological reality.

During imprint vulnerability, existing ego structures become more fluid, and the brain circuitry becomes more open and malleable toward new impressions and imprints. Imprinting or re-imprinting is more likely to occur during periods of high levels of ecstasy, uncertainty, existential transcendence, or external shock, all of which can trigger circuits 5-8. Any such exposure can also destabilize us physically, emotionally, mentally and socially as well.

Communication

Now, one of the main issues facing all of us on a daily basis, and facing the author regarding this very book, is one we are all familiar with: *communication*. As RAW has noted with his "Snafu Principle," communication is only possible between equals. What that means is that, if you are sending a fourth circuit signal, and a person is receiving on his first circuit, this is a cross-up and it is a certainty that there will be a misunderstanding. A more glaring example would be a message sent from someone broadcasting on their seventh circuit, directed at someone who receives it, and tries to interpret it with, their third circuit. It will be very easy for this third circuit individual to dismiss what they are hearing as mystical garbage (or worse), and likewise, the metaprogrammer will likely decide it is not even worth their time to attempt continued communication, as this person is obviously a hopeless yokel. A more ridiculous scenario involves a neurosomatically turned-on individual trying to convey their state-of-mind to a dyed-in-the-wool conservative operating on their second circuit, which will go nowhere very quickly, for obvious reasons. This was one of the primary dichotomies we found ourselves stuck with in the sixties, for example. If one is attempting to communicate with someone whose reality-tunnel is, not wildly different, but even different just to a modest degree, there could be disastrous consequences depending on what is on the line. Everyone knows we don't seek to contradict or challenge those above us on the totem pole; you don't, for example, offer a joint to the person conducting your job interview (more often than not), and you usually don't chastise your boss for any reason. It goes the other way, as well. Those who are able to do so tend not to discuss the merits of Kierkegaard at a sports bar during the big game.

Ultimately, we are only ever really able to properly communicate with people who are at our own level. And that generally leaves a hell of a lot of people out. For someone who has gained facility with their neuroelectric circuit, reality can be a bit isolated, if not lonely. For someone who has gone beyond that, a comrade would basically be a tiny distant island in a very large sea. In taking all this into consideration, it is important to realize that when it comes to human communication, it doesn't really matter what the truth is—for practical purposes. What matters is what people are able to understand in a strictly pragmatic way, and if you direct signals at others who do not understand at all, they may feel threatened in some sense, and quite possibly become at least somewhat hostile. Politicians understand this all too well, but it is quite easy to forget and become frustrated. Just remember that there are probably people out there with whom one can connect; one has only to find them.

As RAW noted, "Intelligence is the capacity to receive, decode and transmit information efficiently. Stupidity is blockage of this process at any point. Bigotry, ideologies, etc. block the ability to receive; robotic reality-tunnels block the ability to decode or integrate new signals; censorship blocks transmission." This definition applies to just about every behavior and activity we see in society, and it's a good one to keep in mind.

Realization

The seventh (neuroelectric) circuit recapitulates the theory of relativity, especially time dilation and the corollary $E=mc^2$. The eighth (neuroatomic) circuit recapitulates quantum mechanics, especially Bell nonlocality. When one imprints these circuits and has even a cursory knowledge of physics, these theories are illuminated and illustrated in an overpowering and affirmative fashion. The structural functionality of the mind mirrors that of the reality of modern physics. The realization that the innermost mind and the outermost universe are identical (or at least, in less strong language, wholly complementary) should not be taken lightly. This waypoint for awareness brings into focus very largely the platitude we've all heard that "all is one." Parroting this slogan, or believing in it casually, is all well and good, but existentially realizing what it means is another matter entirely. Experiencing with one's own being that the laws of physics of the outside world are the same laws of physics that run a person's consciousness is overpowering and unforgettable. Well, one may forget the details. But as I have mentioned, the quantum notions from class become fully reified, as these abstract, dry principles become identical with one's very self! One comes face to face with the infinite, and some may even go beyond it.

Awareness

The "higher" circuits are active in the subconscious at a baseline level at all times, which one realizes upon ratcheting up the energy of the nervous system by whatever means—the perspective shifts so radically that one can see it was happening the whole time. So we are conscious of these processes, but not necessarily aware of them most of the time. That may seem a strange way to put it, but I distinguish between consciousness and awareness. Consciousness is the basic bedrock of nature; everything arises from it, and returns to it, continually. It is, in the most fundamental sense, being. Awareness is more a kind of self-consciousness. When consciousness orients itself in such a way as to reflect upon itself, the phenomenon of awareness arises. Now, fundamental to the concept of the Eight Circuit Model is the understanding of what happens regarding the awareness. For example, one can be aware on one's third circuit only, yet all other circuits are actually firing constantly, subconsciously, even though the awareness you call "you" is only cognizant of the functions of the third circuit. Re-routing the awareness into higher channels is how one becomes more fully conscious of the higher circuits. The machinery one uses for metaprogramming, for example, is constantly in operation in one's brain. When the electric field of the body and brain reach a certain intensity, for some reason the awareness surges into the metaprogramming capacity, and one becomes super-conscious of one's neurological equipment, even to the degree of being able to control it in an intentional—and *aware*—way. Once one ascends to the nonlocal eighth circuit, any convenient distinction between consciousness or subconsciousness and awareness falls away totally. In a very real sense, higher consciousness is not some magical place elsewhere. It all happens right here, right now.

The key in activating the "higher" neurological circuits is in re-routing one's ordinary perception, one's primary waking consciousness—what I have called the awareness—into and through what is normally the subconscious mind. Consciousness on higher circuits is consciousness that has been channeled through what are normally not consciously experienced processes governing the operation of the brain. These circuits are running all the time; most people are simply not aware of them to any sufficient degree. A yogic adept, for example, is conscious of a greater portion of his fundamental experience than a Wall Street executive, probably. The former, presumably through strict discipline and advanced meditative practice, has made fully conscious more of what is normally a subconscious or unconscious mind—of which the latter is, probably more often than not, totally unaware. Once you become suddenly aware of these processes that most people have no idea about, such ideas as those presented in this book begin to make a lot more sense. As psychologist Carl Jung noted wonderfully, "Until you make the unconscious conscious, it will direct your life and you will call it fate." This book is all about making the unconscious or subconscious a conscious, aware process, so that we are no longer governed by a determined fate, but rather can re-route our perception into these more fundamental pathways in order to determine our own fate and join our own minds to the cosmic mind of nature, once and for all.

The Dialectic as a Spectrum

The psychology of Aristotelian logic and the Hegelian dialectic is based essentially upon the function of the rational-mental-symbolic circuit. Quantum psychology is based essentially upon the spectral nature and many possibilities (or probabilities) of the neuroelectric-metaprogramming circuit. The nature of circuit 3 function is dialectical. We unite theses and antitheses into syntheses. These syntheses are further theses to be wedded with other theses and antitheses, and so on, which could apparently go on forever. This is basically all we're doing when we use our rational-mental circuit, though it gets extremely complex and this is not meant to trivialize its richness.

Metaprogramming alters this picture immensely. Instead of a polar, two-option-oriented, end-of-the-spectrum arrangement, metaprogramming awareness opens up every value of the spectrum for access and meaning. That is, third-circuit Aristotelian logic exists at the poles of a duality, and seventh circuit awareness gives values at every point along that spectrum. This configuration is what quantum theory uses—it is probabilistic, spectral, many-valued. It opens up the nature of perspective quite dramatically. Instead of 100% and 0% for an answer, we could have 37%, 62%, 89%, or anywhere in between. Nature seems to jibe with this type of spectral arrangement much more than it does with the Aristotelian, which deals in certainties. Quantum psychology, so named by RAW, deals in uncertainties, or to put it more amusingly, in "maybes." As he noted, if you can say "maybe" instead of "I know, I'm sure, I'm certain," you've gone a long way toward becoming a saner person and a greater lover of the truth. And we could use a lot more of that in this world.

Interplay

Thought and emotion are very, very deeply connected. It is virtually impossible for someone to have an emotion, and not have a corresponding mental state, and it is also virtually impossible to have a thought that does not generate some sort of emotion. When one is talking about one, one is necessarily talking about the other as well. This mirrors the nature of all of the circuits. I have been discussing them individually, but really they all work together for the organism in an organic, coherent whole. One must think of the eighth circuit, not so much as the highest, but as the most fundamental. It informs and gives essence and function to all of the circuits. When one watches a movie, for example, all of the circuits may be functioning in unison; the first, second, third and fourth could all be reacting and interrelating throughout the narrative of the film. If the film is any good, the higher circuits could be stimulated as well, at least subconsciously. One example of a movie that does this is Kubrick's *2001: A Space Odyssey*. Such a wonderful work, it activates all of the circuits, at one time or other, throughout the length of the film. During the "Dawn of Man" sequence, we have: 1. Survival issues, as the apes are on the edge of starvation and in danger of attack from predators; 2: Territorial issues, as the watering hole is contested by two different packs; 3: Mental issues, as Moonwatcher discovers the use of tools; and then later on, 4. The question of the morality of keeping the discovery of the moon Monolith a secret from the public. I will leave it to the interested reader to discover, or think about, Kubrick's presentation of the higher circuits as the Jupiter mission unfolds. It is important to realize that each circuit generally affects every other; while one may possibly only have awareness on one circuit, all circuits are in constant interplay with each other.

A Key Observation

The "higher" circuits of the Eight Circuit Model are emphatically *not* evolutionary. The "lower" four *are*. In order to activate the higher circuits, neurological signals tune into extant but (typically) perceptually inactive pathways in a physical rather than biological process. This implies, of course, that the higher circuits have always existed fundamentally, and did not evolve biologically into existence to pave the way for space migration, as some have claimed. While it may be the case, possibly, that future evolution, if there continues to be a future for man, would incorporate the higher circuits and give them a more central role, it appears that space migration for humans as currently constituted is not necessarily written into our DNA. If the higher circuits are indeed more of a physical than biological phenomenon, it is also implied that, for example, a dog possesses higher circuits, at least in what would appear to us a proto- form. I, for one, have no problems philosophically with these implications. It may be a kind of chauvinism that some of us think humans are the only organisms that could possibly possess the full complement of neurological and trans-neurological circuits, and though it is quite possible that their expression in humans is the most sophisticated that exists on Earth, it is my experience that communication on higher circuits is possible between man and other species. This may be the result of the nature of electrical pathways in the vertebrate or mammalian brains, or I could be wrong, but the foregoing is the result of personal observation.

Explicate Levels

When I say I think the circuits delineated by the Eight Circuit Model are at bottom a result of inherently physical rather than primarily biological processes, I do not mean they are any less fundamental—they are in fact all the more so. I mean that, in a sense, each one is generated by and made up of, or energized by, the next highest, and that the "highest"—the eighth—is actually the most fundamental. So that we see, for example, the metaprogramming circuit, which has to do with electromagnetic phenomena, specifically the conscious visualization of relativity and the speed of light, in turn opens out of—or is in a sense composed of—the nonlocal quantum circuit. When you think about it, this makes a lot of sense. The quantum realm gives rise to and informs the electromagnetic realm of mass-energy. This is precisely the concept behind the notion of the implicate order. In turn, the electromagnetic apparatus of the brain, which we tune into on the neuroelectric circuit, manipulates all of the "classical," or seemingly deterministic, functions of the nervous system and the rest of the body. What we see in the neurological continuum is identical to what the physics community has discovered scientifically—only it is through a conscious agency of the brain. This of course pertains to the basic and fundamental identity without and within the conscious individual, and illustrates the basic unity of man and nature.

Subconscious

I believe that the subconscious mind is actually conscious, but that our normal waking consciousness simply does not have access to it. Despite Copenhagen, the rest of the universe actually exists, independently of human perception, since all nature is a conscious process and imbued with actual being. There are aspects of ourselves of which we are not aware that have some inherent awareness that does not necessarily intersect with our own awareness all of the time, or even, really, much of the time. Bohmian mechanics shows us that a human observer does not, through some spooky unmeasurable process, collapse the wavefunction, but rather the wavefunction only appears to collapse because, in the words of Schrödinger, we are asking a discontinuous question of nature through our limited instruments. So we get a discontinuous answer.

We now know that nature itself is a conscious process, and that, just as in Many-worlds, the wavefunction does not need to undergo a splintering and re-forming, initiated by human consciousness, in order for events to take place. Even if one assumes that consciousness is necessary for a breakdown of the wavefunction, nature—atoms, molecules, photons—has its own fundamental awareness and could collapse the wavefunction itself, if you want to think of it that way. However, the process of superposition and collapse is much more nuanced than all that, which is the reality of the unbroken implicate order, but it would take us rather far afield to go too deeply into that now. Suffice it to say, things can exist, on their own, without a human observer! This may seem like common sense, but it in fact violates the dominant principles of the Copenhagen interpretation!

In any case, this leaves room for my premise, which is that the subconscious mind has an awareness of its own, and it functions perfectly well in the absence of our knowing. What is happening is that, when we activate a higher circuit, our normal waking awareness is joining with our more fundamental subconscious mind, and we become finally aware of the true self that drives us, and that potentially we may shape. Clearly, it is important to understand the reality of the implicate order, for it is a guide that can serve us all well as we seek to plumb the depths of our being, and those of nature.

Unfortunately, it is a common notion that whatever is not being observed should be relegated to the category of nonexistence. That is, the notion is that nothing exists unless or until it has been observed. This is, as I shall point out, not true. Objectively, everything exists, whether it is under the observation of a human or not. We should think of this very much as we think of the subconscious mind, which is by definition not under observation, but is really running the show. Objects existing *out there*, unseen, should be viewed similarly—they exist in the subconscious of the universe. Which, I might add, is also a fundamental part of the human subconscious. Perhaps there is in fact no real division there, in reality.

Space Migration

It is not necessary to incorporate concepts of space migration in a consistent formulation of the Eight Circuit Model. Back in the 1960s, 70s, 80s and 90s, space travel was the rage, and seen by many, possibly even the majority, as the next phase of evolution, even with an immediacy and what seemed an obvious quality of inevitability. Now, almost to 2020, things have changed a lot. Space migration is at best a distant goal, and it appears that, with technology as it is, especially pertaining to propulsion techniques, it could be many, many decades before serious space migration could be remotely possible. No government—or business—on Earth really has the money to engage in large-scale space operations. There are companies and governments with plans for space missions, but these are rather small-scale compared to the point at which people thought we would be right now fifty years ago. No one has walked on the moon—or even been out of low Earth orbit—since 1972. If it were advantageous, feasible and inevitable, we would have been back long ago. More than that, it is very difficult to think of a pressing reason to go. We now realize that there is no scientific justification for exploring space; it would not tell us a thing we don't already know. So what's left? Romance and adventure, and the longing for union through it. It was, back in the decades mentioned, a reasonable expectation to have that the space accomplishments of the sixties and seventies were indicative of an upward spiral into full colonization of local space. But we see now that the truth has turned out to be a bit different. After all, rocketing our squishy, needy, water-filled flesh suits around, with all the life support it takes, seems somewhat ridiculous when you stop and think about it. We can accomplish with robotic probes everything that we could with live humans.

So, perhaps, it is the destiny, not of ours, but of A.I. entities, if that revolution takes place, to physically explore the cosmos. It seems at this point rather improbable that we as a species will be able or willing to engage in large-scale space colonization adventures for a very long time. I mention all this because it points to the truth of my opening statement—it does not at this point appear that space migration is programmed into our DNA in reality. We really don't have a place among the stars, or rather cannot possibly for many decades. In my opinion, more evolved beings, such as possibly A.I., will undertake such missions.

The eight circuits are not *for* space migration. They are not properly *for* anything. They exist in all of us, right now, and it would be more profitable to learn how to use them than to worry about going to Mars, or having people live there, for whatever reason. I consider myself a creature of the future, but it is wiser to focus on the present than on some distant, less than ideal possibility. We have plenty to focus on here without spending hundreds of billions on an adventure with little upside. By all indications, we are, as currently constituted, meant for life on Earth, not among the stars.

Visionaries

Perhaps chemically imbalanced souls—those with mania, schizophrenia, clinical depression, acute psychosis, etc.—get taken out of consensus reality (i.e. normal awareness) to a sufficient degree that they are able to see, with their altered perceptions, how truly limited it is and how extraordinary alternative realities can be. Subjects such as those dealt with in this book, i.e. those which are considered fringe, or mystical, or psychedelic, or visionary, or what have you, are often identified with those who suffer from some sort of psychosis. Indeed, every psychedelic or psychotropic substance known to man has latent psychosis-inducing effects, and the sort of people who are interested in all this are often grouped into the "nutcase" or "crazy" category, and summarily dismissed. So there is a very close correspondence between spiritual apotheosis and insanity. There is clearly some sort of phenomenological link here. Perhaps this sort of phenomenon is what enables so many of the mentally ill to have creative gifts and visionary perspectives. Blake, Byron, Van Gogh, Dickinson, Cobain, etc. were, despite a great deal of suffering, all able to tap into some wellspring of spiritual and visionary insight, and I would wager that the majority of the ideas presented in this book would have resonated with them appreciably.

What is going on here? Are the spiritual adepts worthless for being crazy? Or are the average citizens debilitated for not having any spiritual awareness? As Alan Watts pointed out, there can be prodigious value in psychotic experience. I suppose it all comes down to how open one's mind is, and to have it closed as tightly as so many people do is, I feel, not especially sane.

Magick

The practice of magick is often associated with the phenomena I have been describing, especially by someone like RAW, and for very good reason. Magick is often seen as superstitious or mystical, and dismissed by most people who come into contact with it, usually via the printed word. But this is really a bunch of hot air on the part of people who don't realize how closed their minds are. Magick, defined succinctly, consists simply in executing one's will in order to cause Nature to conform to it. It's that simple. Every time you do that, you're performing an act of magick. Yes, there are people out there in the O.T.O. or the Freemasons engaging in esoteric, arcane rituals that may not make much sense to most people, and seem like a lot of hoopla. It is quite possible that they are not. But insofar as magick is exercised in their rituals, it is not necessarily sensible to dismiss it as something worthless and silly.

Once one gains facility with one's seventh and eighth circuits, one finds one is engaged in magickal acts constantly. Simple, routine behaviors you've been engaging in all your life, looked at and understood properly, would reveal themselves as magickal if one cared to understand why. People look on Aleister Crowley as a charlatan, conman, Satan-worshipper, snake oil salesman, etc., etc. If one were actually to research the man, one would find that he was a perfectly sensible, mild-mannered, affable genius who discovered more in one lifetime about man's place in nature than the Holy Inquisition did in six hundred years. He was chiefly interested in how to exercise his will for good and love, and said so all his life. I'll say it again: Magick, defined succinctly, consists simply in executing one's will in order to cause Nature to conform to it. That is what this book is all about. Or put another way: This book is interested in illustrating that man and nature can conform to one another, for mutual gain. That's magick.

The Model

I'm very much in favor of the notion—the *model*—that all of our mental constructs, all of our ideas and ways of perceiving the world—are models. But I do not feel that model-making is arbitrary. If we are to be accurate or relevant, we cannot be wholly free in making or choosing our constructs. There is a reality, a truth, on which these models must be based, and therefore, while the models are inherently subjective, I feel there is some sort of correspondence there with the objective as well. It is not known whether or not discoverability has an endpoint. Some feel we may be on the verge in physics of what is known as a TOE—a "theory of everything." This potential equation or set of equations would summarize and explain all phenomena of nature, and there could be nothing beyond it as far as objective knowledge is concerned. It would be the endpoint of the enterprise of science as we know it.

Others contend that nature is like an infinite onion—peel back one layer, and there are more and more layers, forever. We peel off classical mechanics, and in its place we find relativity. We peel that back, and we find quantum theory. We peel that back and...what? Do we find hidden variables? Do we discover that the quantum of action is in fact divisible? And what could be beyond that? So, in reality, the truth is out there, and it corresponds to an objective way that things are. Perhaps physicists will soon be out of a job, or perhaps they never will. But our models, then, cannot be just what we'd like them to be. In our imaginations we can dream up anything; but when we're talking physics, or mathematics, or computer science, or the Eight Circuit Model, even though our models are molded by subjective human minds, there must be some resonance there with a natural order of things. And eventually, subject and object are one...

CIRCUIT 5

A Holistic Circuit

The fifth circuit is imprinted by intense ecstatic experience via biological or chemical means. It processes mind-body (neurosomatic) feedback loops, which have the tendency to generate sensory bliss or feeling "high." Christian Science, NLP, holistic medicine and cannabis are known to initiate temporary forays along this circuit; more advanced meditation techniques, especially Tantra, are in part designed to create a more lasting awareness and presence in this state.

Everything we see, smell, hear, touch, taste, think—everything we perceive—is a signal that impinges on a brain and nervous system grounded in awareness. We usually think of mind and body as separate, but when we realize the aforementioned, this isn't quite tenable. The nervous system extends throughout the body, from the brain to the eyes, nose, ears, tongue, to the tips of our toes and everywhere in between, and back again to the brain. But what is the brain? It is a fleshy organ inside our skull, right? How does one separate that from the rest of the body? Without a constant supply of blood, the brain dies. Without input from all of these other nerves, the brain malfunctions or shuts down. Awareness of the totality of the body, including the brain and mind, and proper control, use of the body, and positive somatic programming (e.g. feeling "high"), represent the primary functions of the fifth "neurosomatic" circuit.

This circuit is in a sense holistic, in that the body becomes one with itself, and potentially the environment, to at least some degree. The faith healing (often "miraculous"), bliss, ecstasy, rapture, etc. we have heard about down through history and still today are really the result of positive imprints on the fifth circuit. Sadly, just as easily a negative imprint can be made, causing terrifying nightmares for some people—a kind of schizophrenia. Neurosomatic consciousness can be achieved through yogic pranayama, which is an advanced breathing technique with origins in the East, and also cannabis, which, probably beneficially, overall, is becoming more acceptable and mainstream in the West, being by now legal for recreational consumption in many American states. Cannabis releases neurotransmitters that, when bound at the proper synapses, alter the electromagnetic field of the brain in such a way as to trigger neurosomatic consciousness. Judicious use of this substance is not a bad thing, if done responsibly, but for anyone unwilling to try it, all is not lost. Pot consumption only activates this circuit *temporarily*; it takes a bit more work and experience to gain a more meaningful and lasting sense of what this type of awareness is all about. Onward and upward.

Neurosomatic Methods

Positive neurosomatic experiences are quite accessible and open the door to a whole new experience of reality. RAW points out that pranayama will "remove all forms of depression, including profound grief and bereavement; it will soothe anger and remove resentments; it seems beneficial to all minor health problems and—occasionally—major health problems. Hindus, who are professionals at pranayama, claim a great deal more, such as immunity to pain of all sorts [and] *samadhi*..." Samadhi is a state of "union with God" in Hindu philosophy, and can be achieved at advanced levels of yogic meditative practice. (It involves circuits yet to come; more later.) As previously mentioned, this circuit can also be experienced upon the ingestion of cannabis, whose effects are well-known. There is a real enrichment of perception, in which colors, tastes, sounds are all greatly magnified and made richer and more fully appreciable. There is also enhanced feeling, a real sensory and sensual cascade leading to hedonic bliss and being "high." These are all perfectly normal phenomena at this level of consciousness.

Another wonderful way to experience a neurosomatic high is through skiing. As gravity takes over and you engage in what is essentially a controlled fall, enjoying the crisp mountain air and the fluffiness of the snow, shooshing and turning effortlessly among evergreens and aspen while rushing down the mountain, a real sense of weightless bliss can be the result. While not always as reliable a method as the previous two, I personally have experienced this sensation numerous times while skiing, and it is clearly the easiest method, for anyone with the time and means to do it. For hours afterward you experience a kind of contented glow, though this can be a little offset by sore muscles!

Less accessible ways to turn on this circuit are sensory deprivation or isolation (although floatation tanks are becoming a little more mainstream), and the microgravity experienced by astronauts. The former three methods are obviously more favorable, and for anyone not interested in cannabis or skiing, there is a universe of information and options out there for studying pranayama. Don't watch a youtube video—learn from a master. If you've never tried it, I guarantee that if you go in with an open mind, you won't regret it! There is an unfortunate dark side to this circuit as well, however. Negative imprints, or psychosis, can lead to sensory experience being deeply painful; general discomfort throughout the body that cannot be assuaged; disorganized and often terrifying perceptions; and crippling, horrible anxiety. This is often, as we know, the experience of many schizophrenics, but in fact this syndrome can occur in anyone who has had severe trauma involving their fifth circuit. Amateur seekers, heavy pot users, and of course anyone with a family history of schizophrenia, are all unfortunately susceptible to these grim nightmares. That said, we shall, going forward, focus on the good, which seems to outweigh for most people the latter.

A Personal Revolution

Those who have activated and gained proficiency with their fifth circuit tend to be less interested in established social networks and more interested in self-discovery, particularly of the body and the mind's relationship with it. They tend to be more interested in people who have made the same discoveries that they have, and to shun an establishment which they see as cold and mired in backwardness and overly conservative mores. Hence we see the phenomenon of the hippies in the 1960s, and the counterculture(s) of today. Some see fifth circuit awareness as the beginning of the true self. This is the realm of sensory pleasure, of rapture, of the beginnings of true bliss. Of the suspension of social imprints. Such sensations felt for the first time offer a personal revolution, and a revelation that there can be much more to existence than meets the eye.

Intelligent Manipulation of the Body

The turned-on artist typifies awareness on this circuit, as does the Karate master or the Eastern yogi. Tantra is another well-known method of activating it, as well as ecstatic dance. Sports of all sorts are also a prime example. And psychedelic chemicals, particularly cannabis. What has historically enabled explorations into this form of self-development is simple: leisure. Time to do it, unencumbered by lower-circuit concerns. When survival pressures are eased or relieved, the luxuries of self-actualization and neurological exploration become possible.

Leary writes that activating the fifth circuit involves "the intelligent manipulation of the Body freed from the demands and limitations of terrestrial-territorial hives. The control of one's own physiology. The aesthetic-eroticization of sensation and motion. The Fifth Self-Actualization; learning how to use the body as Time-Machine, as feed-back rapture instrument." The body is no longer totally robotic, as it surely is the majority of the time when operating exclusively on the lower circuits—which are most always on auto-pilot. The four-brained individual can be seen essentially as an automaton, screening in a very narrow range for relevant behavioral cues and reacting to stimuli according to deep conditioning and static imprints.

Certain Hindu, Buddhist/Tantric and Sufi schools taught that the path to expanded consciousness and higher intelligence involved a redirecting of awareness through the body-mind. These teachings were often secret or highly abstract because of the outrage such practices cause in terms of hive concepts of sin and social responsibility. They deeply offend yokels. Most systems of popular morality involve some notion that sensual-somatic or hedonic pleasures are somehow wrong, move one away from the common good of society, and are thus taboo. We hope such taboos can be set aside.

General Awareness

Based purely on an estimate by myself, it would seem that a conservative projection for the number of people who have some appreciable fifth circuit awareness, or have had it in the past, is around ten percent of the population. That is, about ten percent of people out there can make sense of the statements in this section of the book, and roughly that many people have moved at least a little bit out of their four-circuit robotism. In every population, there is a minority that is "turned on" so to speak. As one moves to increasingly higher circuits, the proportion of people to whom the pertinent knowledge makes good sense winnows to a smaller and smaller figure. That we have maybe ten percent of people who have some understanding of the fifth circuit is both good and bad; good, in the sense that that is rather a lot of people; bad, in the sense that there are hundreds of millions who still have no concept that they are basically very unaware robotic (though conscious) mechanisms, and have no knowledge of notions that ideally one would like everyone to know. C'est la vie.

There seems to be an assumption among some writers and thinkers that progress will ameliorate this and, one day, we'll all be eight-circuit adepts. I see things a bit differently. Throughout history, there has been a core group—maybe one or two percent of the population—that really holds the light for human civilization, a group that is compassionate, wise, caring, conscientious, philosophically adept, thoughtful, and committed to excellence. These people usually have some appreciable knowledge of the higher circuits, which is often presented or encoded in arcane, secret or occult language. While the population of the planet has grown, and this class of people has necessarily gotten a little bigger, it has remained at a baseline of a very small portion of the general populace. Fifth circuit awareness is the doorway to this knowledge, so we will hope, as more people get turned on, that more and more people really do leave some of their automatic reflex behind; historically though, the evidence is that, while it is promising, most people who achieve neurosomatic awareness will remain there, or fall back. This seems to be the unfortunate reality. But I suppose ten percent at least at this level is a lot better than nothing. Perhaps I'm wrong and we'll see some sort of appreciable linear increase in this figure. I hope so.

Sacred Bequests

The greatest gifts to humanity have been those souls who have experienced the broad vistas of the higher circuits and brought them back to us in the form of art: poetry, prose, music, painting and sculpting, films, theater, etc. It is one thing to be a mystic experiencing bliss and insight on his fifth (or higher) circuit; it is quite another to be able to translate that experience into third circuit programs that can be comprehended by the majority. Intuition is very important here; the mystic or artist has a very strong intuitive faculty, as this is the hallmark of higher-circuit experience, but then the artist is able to encode signals in his or her work that exercise the intuition of the audience, creating a transmission that originates and terminates in some degree of higher consciousness. I think it's safe to say that people like Beethoven, Picasso, Dali, Poe, Blake, Carroll were adepts at this. Anyone who has truly seen the work of Dali understands how forbidden his paintings are, and that to view his work properly is rather to gaze into the face of God, but one also has to conclude that these signals are perceived at least by the subconscious of many people who have never had an appreciable awareness of the present subject. These notions indicate why such people seem to flock to the arts as a profession or hobby; a few also have become great scientists, like Newton, Einstein, Bohr, Schrödinger and Feynman. There are particular resonances, as we shall discuss, between quantum mechanics and eighth circuit awareness, for example. But before I get too far ahead, I must stress that anyone can experience the genius of such luminaries. Their work was a doorway for me personally to enter this realm, and we must treasure their bequests to us—they are sacred.

Diamonds in the Rough

Fifth circuit adepts are usually akin to diamonds in the rough. While the majority is struggling with body problems, emotional problems, mental problems, and social problems (often involving guilt), the neurosomatic grace of a turned-on individual seems to wash this all away, leading to a serene contentment, a "glow" even, that is basically alien to the majority. Feeling good goes a long way toward transcending the persistent difficulties encountered on the lower circuits, and a person who experiences the world with this sort of detachment is often quite copacetic in situations where other people might be really miserable. There is definitely a degree of freedom involved in prolonged fifth circuit awareness that is not available to people who have no knowledge of or experience with it. This may all sound unbelievable, but don't knock these ideas until you've had some real-world contact with them. Neurosomatic turn-on really does create a new and improved experience of the world; if one can manage to sustain it, one has gained a 'quantum jump' on the rest of society. Suddenly, all the little things that get people—the meaningless bullshit—don't seem so important anymore. In truth, such awareness is quite liberating, and brings much more meaning, and possibly purpose, into one's life.

Lasting Effects

Most people who activate their neurosomatic circuit only do so in flashes—for temporary periods, after which time they fall back to a more conventional consciousness. There are those, however, who have a more or less constant awareness on this circuit. Given a favorable imprint and the right circumstances, one can work one's way toward a constant fifth circuit state. Such a scenario can be brought into being through various forms of meditation—the Jnana, Bhakti, Karma and Raja yogas in Hinduism, as well as the more Buddhist flavors, like Tantric Buddhism, practiced perhaps most powerfully in Tibet and Nepal. There are of course many variants of these practices in the East, but they are all directed in some sense toward achieving fifth circuit proficiency, and of course higher circuits as well once the former is mastered.

While it is (happily) not an option for most, psychosis of various kinds can also lead to full fifth circuit awareness. Mental illnesses, such as manic-depression or schizophrenia, and all of their various and sundry variants, can, and frequently do, generate a more or less constant neurosomatic consciousness. Aside from this, accidents of genetics and/or environment, with a little luck thrown in, can enable certain people to achieve this state as well.

The point to recognize is that it is possible to energize this circuit on a permanent basis, as many people have done it. The meditative schools are clearly the most promising and accessible for most people, and with commitment and resolve, they are infinitely effective. As an aside, the taking of drugs usually does not lead to full awareness on a permanent basis, but for most people only creates temporary periods of this awareness until one ceases to administer the drug. It seems nature discourages cheating.

Changing Brains, Changing Minds

The physical sensations of the body are really qualia of the brain; the neural interface between body and brain constitutes the neurosomatic circuit. Mastery of this circuit is a kind of "hack" — or one could even potentially call it a sort of metaprogramming of the body. Naturally, mastery of this circuit could confer many hedonic advantages. When we are without neurosomatic awareness, we are on a kind of dull auto-pilot, and we are basically slaves to our bodies, with very little awareness of them. Pain and anxiety are much less pronounced and much more under control if the neurosomatic circuit is firing, and as RAW pointed out, we can even significantly reduce rates of illness, and generally feel much better and much more alive. Without this awareness, we really have no insight into the fact that brain and body are one indivisible unit, and our consciousness of our bodies, minds and selves is severely attenuated as compared with the former higher state of mind and being. Sadly, in such a fractured and unhealthy society as ours, most people do not have the opportunities or really the time to explore their bodies or to focus on how they can become more aware and fully alive in general. We live in a sick society, and without fifth circuit know-how, we shall remain that way.

As I have pointed out elsewhere, the proportion of people who have attained this awareness at one time or other is appreciable but relatively small, and this does not bode well for suggestions of meaningful change. I do hope it is in some way enough that you are reading these words right now, as the only way change ever occurs is by changing one mind at a time. A society of neurosomatically turned-on people would be freer and happier, but that, I know, is a lot to ask. Hopefully I, and you, can change a mind or two.

CIRCUIT 6

DNA

DNA is a physical molecule, but it codes information. DNA is essentially an intelligence, and in aggregate, is the smartest and most powerful intelligence currently on planet Earth. It has goals and employs strategies far beyond the scope of the individual, or even really any specifiable group of individuals. As we go forward we will talk about the noosphere, which is the morphological or morphogenetic field encompassing all Earth intelligence—plant and animal life, chemistry and human culture—which are all influenced or defined by the properties of DNA. This genetic wizardry exists in every cell of every living organism and sends out instructions, via RNA, to construct, preserve, and propagate itself—as it has through every single epoch for around four billion years. Every living creature, from ferns to fungi to tyrannosaurs to used car salesmen, is a kind of robot programmed by DNA to perform specific functions in the ecosystem, the chief one being reproduction and the continuation of the "life" of the DNA master tape. All of this constitutes an overarching biological (and also cultural) intelligence that basically operates the planet. This is sometimes called "Gaia" but I have chosen the term "noosphere" which I extend from human cultural activity to the entire living intelligence of the planet in general. Evolution unfolds in an unpredictable and partially free but nonrandom way in the cocoon of this intelligence. Awareness of all of this was a part of the human experience in many cultures until the onset of sedentism, when gradually but forcefully it was lost. There has been a rekindling of Gaia awareness in recent decades, but it is still considered a fringe belief. As the future unfolds, and if we survive as a species, this is bound to change.

The Language of Life

Having activated this circuit, one becomes aware of the nervous system's reception of signals directly from DNA. The nervous system continually receives DNA-RNA dialogue signals, which contain the record of the genetic chain going all the way back to the beginning—to the origin of life on this planet. It is suggested that there is a nonlocal feedback mechanism between the DNA information field and the noosphere, which reflects and to some extent coordinates all intelligent processes on the planet. When the sixth circuit becomes active, the signals from DNA become conscious. At this stage, many thousands of genetic memories may flash by, revealing the record of all Earth evolution. It is now known that neurons can re-write their own DNA; we can extend this knowledge to say that the communication between a neuron and its own DNA may constitute a more general process. Leary points out that, once proficiency is reached in deciphering the DNA-RNA conversation, it will be seen that all organic life is essentially a complex, unified language system.

Evolution and Superhumanity

The sixth circuit begins to consciously operate when the awareness gains access to signals within individual neurons in the brain, creating a feedback between the electromagnetic neural mind-field and the DNA-RNA dialogue. In other words, at this level we become conscious of the genetic script. The DNA archive becomes fully available to the individual in a waking state, and opens up vast vistas for conscious exploration. There have been harbingers throughout history of what became Darwin's codified theory of evolution, and this was made possible by the fact that genetic consciousness is a neurological reality.

It is worth noting here, however, that past authors have made a mistake when they attribute Nietzsche's forecast of superhumanity to the neurogenetic circuit, at least as far as Nietzsche himself was concerned. If you look closely at his writings, he was careful to point out that his scheme for the ubermensch was not an evolutionary one. I.e., that this "higher type" would not be a product of advancing biological evolution, but rather a complex set of circumstances involving the evolution of *individuals*. Nietzsche was perhaps referring more to the eighth circuit than the sixth when he made these pronouncements. There is no ready formula for activating the sixth circuit, but it is usually made available to those who are engaged in an intense study of the yogas, particularly Raja yoga, and is famously part of the experience involving psychedelic chemicals. Bio-chemical-electrical stresses and shocks can also be responsible for an imprint here. Experience of this circuit is numinous, highly mystical, and impresses upon the yogi or psychonaut a particular sort of awareness that is unshakeable.

Chaos and Order

Darwin and his ilk certainly did revolutionary work, and perhaps contributed more to the modern scientific paradigm than even the likes of Einstein or Bohr. But in the place of God, whose authority had ruled Christendom for over a thousand years, they instituted a nihilistic blind chance to explain everything we see. Natural selection, for me, is clearly a real process, but I, for one, have a problem with the notion that the mutations which lead to selection are utterly random. If they were, it is logical to assume that no coherent structures would be able to form in the first place, given the infinities of possible chemical interactions that would produce no orderly result. It seems, rather—and there is now some evidence for this—that the mutation process is not entirely random, and indeed I suggest that no physical process in the universe is *truly* random. But that is a digression. Neo-Darwinians and most atheist-materialist types, certain as they are of their personal philosophies, have created a paradigm of meaninglessness and what is to me, essentially, a form of nihilism. I here suggest that evolution is an orderly process, and that while there are a lot of suboptimal species, with suboptimal features, and all sorts of birth defects all the time, etc., etc., there is some subtle principle informing the development of speciation that cannot reasonably be explained as the result of one in a quintillion chance.

The key concept in understanding Nature is *intelligence*. Evolution is not an accident-driven, survival of the fittest, "nasty, brutish, and short"-lived hell that is red in tooth and claw, but rather an increase in intelligence in a cosmic fabric that learns. Leary gives us the beautiful analogy in which matter is the freezing or storing of information, and energy is the movement of quanta of information. The universe is a giant brain. More than that, it is inherently conscious. I don't, however, share Tim Leary's view that DNA contains the master instructions of all evolution from start to finish, for one principal reason: contingency. The state of Earth can change drastically at any time, and while general lines of development are likely in most scenarios, unforeseen adaptations may have to evolve. It strikes me as more elegant that DNA has plasticity, and is not a rote time-script, but rather an intelligent unfolding according to the local implicate order. I do share Leary's discontent with modern, neo-Darwinian theories of evolution, which rely on blind chance as the primary explanation. This seems clearly wrong. None of this addresses, of course, what future, if any, the DNA molecule will have after a certain point in cultural and specifically technological evolution. I think it likely that DNA's future roles as forecast by Leary may take place in an entirely different medium. But we shall have to wait and see.

Awareness

It is fervently hoped that as genetic awareness grows, there will be more humane and empathetic treatment of all denizens of Earth—human, animal and plant life. We as a civilization have a woeful record when it comes to the respect and veneration that all life deserves, and perhaps when we come to understand the evolutionary process more fully, our compassion will grow along with our knowledge. This is crucial if the planet and its citizens are to have health, sanity and happiness. After a certain point, one experiences a feedback loop involving DNA, RNA and the central nervous system, enabling one to consciously tune in to Gaianoosphere intelligence and observe the subtlety behind the evolutionary process, seeing all life as the playful dance of a sacred, ancient principle. This inevitably leads to a wiser, more compassionate attitude toward all living creatures that is sorely needed if the modern age is not to destroy the heritage of billions of years of evolution.

Stewardship

At the current stage of evolution, where time-scales are so short, i.e. change happens so radically so quickly, the agent of evolution has ceased to be biological, species evolution and is now cultural evolution, which for the present purposes is really up to the individual or small groups of individuals. As we now have the science of genetics, and relatedly genetic engineering, we can effect genetic changes much more quickly, deliberately and intentionally in bringing about alterations to the gene pool that might take thousands of years naturally. Evolution is now literally in human hands. What this means, as I mentioned, is that the individual or a small subculture of individuals are the most potent means of lasting change in the world. One person's discovery could radically alter future history in ways that have not been as dramatic historically. Where all of this will lead, vis-à-vis the development of genetics, is impossible to know, and there is no particular reason to be sanguine about it. The changes could just as easily be disastrous as liberating. But change is coming faster and faster, for good or ill. We have reached a stage where DNA intelligence, both internally and externally, is creating a revolution. The noosphere has reached a stage at which an organism whose evolution it has guided now has the means to duplicate and accelerate the process with its own technology, thus taking over stewardship of evolution for good or ill.

Sex and Death

DNA enjoys relative immortality. Humans and other organisms are born, live and die, but the information in DNA has remained intact in an unbroken chain going back 3.8 billion years—not bad longevity. It is hypothesized that, quite possibly, there is some retention, some memory, in the DNA system that is passed along down through the generations, so that, not only do I carry my grandfather's genes, but something of his life up to the point he fathered my mother, as well. Whether or not the reader entertains ideas about reincarnation, this could be some purely physical basis for it, to whatever extent one can entertain it at the present time.

For DNA, both birth and death are absolute necessities. Without multiple lifetimes, it could not fine-tune, adapt, change intelligently—it could not evolve—and moreover, it could not regulate the ecosystem without the inevitability of the death of each and every organism. If no one died, resources for living would disappear, everyone would go extinct, and life would erase itself. No, death is a great fertilizer for continued life, and, as I have noted, makes evolution itself a possibility. And we see a vast web of living relationships built up over the eons—the result of billions of years of evolution, really—that represents an intelligence far surpassing the smartest of humanity. Perhaps if people understood this there would be less of a willingness to allow these age-old yet fragile ecosystems to die in the name of short-term, expedient economic activity. Or perhaps we are not quite evolved enough yet to know how to stop.

The Noosphere

If one considers the levels of intelligence of DNA, one can see a reinforcing, multiple-redundancy built into the whole thing. The individual, who is the agent responsible for reproducing, is one level. The gene pool, which is an aggregate of all the sorts of individuals necessary for tribal functions (and has historically been more rigidly defined), and which, given a large enough population, could survive many dangers even with significant losses, is the next level. The species is the general diffusion of a set of genes across every habitable part of the planet, and is even more resilient and adaptable than the sub-groups at the level of a local gene-pool, making up a higher level still. The ecosystem, a yet higher level, constitutes the interlinked functioning of the biosphere, wherein the various relationships between species are what enable all involved to sustain, based upon the cycling of resources that any one species could not accomplish on its own, the life functions of every other.

And there is, believe it or not, a kind of coordinator overseeing all of this activity which I call the *noosphere*, which is really a combination of the biosphere and the mental-cultural sphere into one vast intelligence making Earth truly one entity. This is a rather abstract idea, but suffice it to say that this noosphere represents a kind of force that underlies all of the relationships on Earth, and tends generally, with a few brief exceptions, to keep them running smoothly and in relative homeostasis. This phenomenon has also been known as the *Gaia* hypothesis. But terminology is not as important as recognition. It is noteworthy that it is this Gaia, or noosphere, that has sustained life on this planet, in an unbroken chain, for almost four billion years. Nature is intelligent, and this noosphere is the local incarnation of this intelligence.

THE NOOSPHERE

The Idea

The term *noosphere* was originally created to refer to the sphere of human mental activity, especially as it pertains to culture, and the effects of culture on the biosphere. I use it here in a more general way to describe both the sphere of mental activity, and the biosphere itself, because in reality there is no dividing line in the planetary intelligence between the two. This intelligence is nonlocally local, and its prime substrate is DNA, although inanimate matter does play a role in the cycles making up this noosphere. The word comes from the Greek *noos* or *nous* for mind, and *sphere* for sphere. As the planet's envelope appears to be of one undivided mind, this terminology seems appropriate.

Whereas some thinkers have separated the biosphere and noosphere, I feel there is in reality no such division. This is more in line with the theorizing along the lines of the "Gaia" hypothesis, in which Earth and all its denizens are one living, wholly interrelated presence, ultimately with one local "mind." I feel the following quotes from *The Archaic Revival* of Terence McKenna are particularly illuminating regarding what I am calling the noosphere, and he has called the "Oversoul":

"The Oversoul is some kind of field that is generated by human beings but that is not under the control of any institution, any government, or any religion. It is actually the most intelligent life form on the planet, and it regulates human culture through the release of ideas out of eternity and into the continuum of history."

"I take very seriously the idea that the Logos is real, that there is a guiding mind—an Oversoul—that inhabits the biome of the planet, and that human balance, dignity, and religiosity depend on having direct contact with this realm. That is what shamanism is providing. It was available in the West until the fall of Eleusis and the Mystery traditions—to some people—but then it was stamped out by barbarians who didn't understand what they had destroyed. The soul of the planet is not neutral about the emerging direction of human history. We are part of a cosmic drama—I really believe that—and although the cosmic drama has lasted for untold ages, I don't think it's going to run for untold ages into the future."

The Morphogenetic Field

This is all deeply tied to the neurogenetic circuit. As noted previously, the first scientific model of this circuit appeared in Sheldrake's *A New Science of Life*. It was assumed by some that certain non-ego-related information, which was known not to be coming from the brain, must have come directly from the genetic material. This picture was, however, not quite right. Sheldrake, a biologist, knew that the genes could not carry such information, and therefore posited a nonlocal field, which is permitted by quantum theory (and which I shall address soon), which he named the *morphogenetic field*. The field communicates between genes, but cannot properly be found in the genes. This is basically one of the major mechanisms of communication and intelligence driving the noosphere. As I have stated, inanimate matter also plays a distinct role in the noosphere primarily in the exquisitely regulated cycles making up the diverse series of ecosystems of the biosphere—which should be thought of as a *level* of the overarching noosphere. This is an essential principle of the Gaia hypothesis. It's an open question just what exact "mechanism," if you will, the noosphere uses for memory, processing and communication. Perhaps it relies on a networking of extant living brains, a local DNA field, or a set of higher-dimensional matrices of some kind, or some combination of the three—or something else entirely. Whatever the case may be, Earth possesses mind. Sadly, by now the human race has mostly forgotten this. I wish it could remember.

(Non) Local Envelope

If one accepts the notion that there is a nonlocal consciousness; that the nonlocal correlations discovered by quantum mechanics are in fact real and constitute a kind of suffusing matrix or network of connections between every point and every other point in the universe and potentially also the multiverse, then it is not a stretch to assume that there is a collective mind operating on Earth. This collective mind operates both locally and universally. The local orientation exists because Earth is specially attuned to itself—signals generated in one Earth entity are decoded easily in the identical or like equipment in other Earth entities; you merely have to tune in or become aware through some event. This phenomenon ties into the larger network because it is self-same; it is just that the signals from deeper in the multiverse are alien and decidedly more on the periphery as compared with the immediacy and familiarity of terrestrial affairs. When one becomes aware of this collective mind operating on Earth, it is unmistakable and the observer harkens immediately back to any mysticism or perhaps Eastern religious notions s/he has picked up in the course of time. One may begin to question it as the memories fade, but one never forgets it and is never quite at peace with the somnambulant state of the planet with regard to these matters. Eventually, Earth will awaken to its potential and to the now hidden truths of existence waiting for us farther down the evolutionary chain.

This envelope is called the *noosphere*, and comprises the totality of the nonlocal quantum network of consciousness—for our purposes, in the vicinity of Earth. When a tipping point has been reached, we will achieve a new level of evolution through a quantum jump in the collective mind of the noosphere. The sixties were a false start in achieving this shift. But they were not random, and they were not an accident—they were evidence of a strategy evolution must employ to achieve this necessary mutation. Evolution is not perfect, and its methods are often coarse, so we had precisely what one would expect: a premature form of the mutation that resulted in relatively little. But if Earth keeps trying, and gets better at engineering these waves so that eventually the momentum creates a lasting change, the mechanism will have been a success—one in a long line in the history of evolution on this planet. The noosphere is pregnant. One day in the not too distant future, there will be a profound transformation of all life on planet Earth.

In the noosphere, all consciousness: from humans, animals, even plants—that of Earth itself—is linked into a collective, unified network that underlies or envelops the entire biosphere. Many mystics and psychonauts have reported tuning into this array, and sensing a unity that exists at a more fundamental level than the everyday. For example, you could be at a good party and observe that all of the partygoers are behaving according to a rhythm that is somehow common to everyone yet is normally beneath the surface. Everyone is him- or herself, but there is a current guiding everyone's activity, and all are in some kind of active union. It is very difficult to describe, and hard and rare to see. When the planet awakens to itself, God only knows what it will be like. And the individual and the collective will be one.

The noosphere is real: it is, fundamentally, a pool of the energy of all citizens of Earth, and it is observable. It is a conscious multiverse of individual minds bound together collectively in a strange but perfectly real organism of neurological space.

Our future depends on its unfettered evolution.

Planetary Mind

Each individual human in society is like a neuron in the cultural meme-system's brain. And this brain constitutes the local noosphere. The noosphere is the nonlocal envelope of Earth consciousness and activity. All thought and culture exist and evolve through it—the collective mind of Earth. Earth is a series of fields upon fields, active information being shared by all sentient beings. Becoming more attuned to it should be a major goal of our kind in this century.

When discussing this phenomenon, people sometimes use the term "collective unconscious" to refer to a global network of an unconscious or subconscious mind suffusing the biosphere and the noosphere—a continuum of shared mind. This is frowned upon by many because it is not at all what Jung meant when he coined the term, but there must be a reason why this term has been appropriated. Though the definition of the term is being violated, it is noteworthy that somehow it feels right to people who have intuitively or explicitly experienced the phenomena of the noosphere.

All minds are interconnected in a vast universal network. The vast majority of the time, there is no awareness of this reality as it is buried deep in the subconscious. But it is nevertheless there, and factors into our relations with other people and even animals significantly. Incidentally, when one becomes aware of this phenomenon it is a very eye-opening experience. It occurs to me, and it is quite a phenomenon to behold, that we truly are of one mind as a planet. Normally this truth is veiled behind a shroud of functional sleepfulness, but one can awaken this awareness through some of the methods we have discussed. What seems to occur is that all minds are in a constant feedback loop of communication with each other, and thoughts that one person has might get reactions from the rest of the group, or vice-versa. It is difficult to describe, and can only really be appreciated when experienced, but upon doing so, one gathers that while in one sense we are all separate, in another, equally valid sense, we are operating in unison as one mind. On what level this feedback occurs—species-wide, planetary, galactic, or universal—I do not venture to guess. But the phenomenon is, needless to say, noteworthy and consequential. It is possible that in the future we will achieve an ideal balance between individual and collective. The individual will still be prized, but will belong meaningfully to a supporting community, the two in an optimal proportion to one another. A more active awareness of these phenomena would, I feel, inevitably bring about such a configuration, which could be in many ways valuable. It seems that this continuum is mostly out of balance throughout much, if not most, of the world. And as I have said, our future as a planet depends on greater awareness along these lines.

CIRCUIT 7

Self-Metaprogramming

The well known cliché "it's all in your mind" captures, really, the essence of metaprogramming consciousness—also associated with the "third eye." This has to do with the notion that everything you see, touch, taste, feel, smell, think, perceive in any way, is experienced through the processing of signals in the network of brain circuitry. This is the true seat of the mind. When one is looking at an apple on the table, one is actually experiencing a subjective projection inside of one's own head. This is where the 'catastrophe of the infinite regress' usually enters the picture. Once you become aware of being aware of the apple, you are metaprogramming, but there's a little hitch—how do you become aware of being aware of being aware of the apple? And once you have done that, how do you become aware of being aware of being aware of being aware of the apple? This could obviously go on forever. That is the catastrophe. I suggest that there is a way out through the recognition of the phenomenon of awareness, which is inherently infinite, but I'll leave it to the reader to decide whether or not to go crazy over this. At the very least, when we truly become aware of the apparatus that is looking at, making a picture of, and consciously perceiving the apple—as distinct from seeing the apple as some static object "out there"—we are becoming cognizant of the fact that everything we experience is taking place inside of our skulls, and the outside world is something of a phantasm. We will revisit this paradox when we talk about the eighth circuit, which offers a resolution of this difficulty which, if we were not careful, could all too easily lead us into solipsism—without sufficient understanding. In any case, being aware of being aware—or being aware of just exactly how one is mentally aware of things—is what this circuit is all about.

This circuit is imprinted by advanced yogas and psychedelic chemicals. It consists of a cybernetic consciousness—i.e., programming one's programming—which enables one to seize awareness of, reprogram and re-imprint all of the other circuits. The conscious choice of true will comes in at this point, making varied options for action almost limitless in certain contexts. This harkens to the multiple universes of Everett's "Many-worlds" hypothesis, in which we may even be able to metaprogram multiple universes. Certainly, at the very least new reality-tunnels become available for use.

Spacetime Super-Reality

The seventh circuit mediates the discovery and use of the brain and nervous system itself as a device for ordering reality—for organizing perception, sensation, feeling, thought, the body as a whole, choice, imagination, etc. This neuroelectric, metaprogramming circuit involves the nervous system's awareness of its own function, causing a greatly expanded capacity for "will," and allowing for a situation in which imprints are no longer random but can be selected and manipulated. It is an understatement to say that this awareness constitutes the very definition of Einsteinian relativity, both in content and in form. One becomes intimately aware of the phenomenon of time-dilation, and illuminatingly cognizant of the famous equivalence principle, whereby $E=mc^2$, in which it is seen that all matter pulses to the rhythm of a subtle vibration, and that all energy is identical with this material pulsation.

At this stage, the electrical pathways of the nervous system are coursing with this energy, which resonates with the awareness to produce that which one experiences in this way. The slow, linear, classical-Newtonian world is obliterated at this point in favor of a high-velocity, multi-faceted, multi-dimensional spacetime super-reality. Historically, descriptions of such perceptions have been attributed to mystics, visionary poets and schizophrenics. The neurological consciousness of "synapse dynamics" is what these figures were experiencing—the brain's recognizing its own electrical intricacies.

Neurological Menu

Circuit 7 can be activated by increasing the energy throughput of the electric highways of the nervous system through various methods including advanced meditation and yoga techniques (including Tantra), mind machines which alter brainwaves, and various neuroelectric chemicals. These methods do not in fact directly stimulate electric activity as one might expect, but rather dissolve synaptic barriers which prevent large-scale signal throughput, thereby increasing the latent energy level of the nervous system. In the same way that the neurosomatic circuit involves an opening of synaptic gates, the neuroelectric circuit is normally kept out of awareness as a subconscious, involuntary process. But when activated or imprinted, one's river of awareness is fully diverted into its channel, and myriads of previously unavailable options are suddenly thrust into one's mind. At the level of this metaprogramming circuit, one becomes aware of one's own brain processes, and accordingly, has a much expanded will because of it. What was once a thought-process based upon only one criterion is now a whole neurological menu of options from which to choose.

Communication

Average people communicate in average, slow, clunky, boring ways. According to Leary, yokel conversation involves things like, "How's the weather? Where's the food? Attack the enemy! Shall we breed? How are the kids? Who is in charge? Is this immoral, illegal or dangerous?" Neurosomatic conversation is a little more sophisticated, being relatively meta-cultural and beyond normal hive chatter, and involving more body-language which is unnoticed below this level. Neuroelectric communication takes place when one brain, moving at high-velocity, communicates with another on the same wavelength, and it happens much more rapidly and with much more information-content than does normal banal speech. It is also the nature of metaprogramming awareness for one signal to carry multiple meanings, as when it reaches the mind it "explodes many mirrored meanings," making what would ordinarily be perceived in only one way generate multiple perspectives. Not only that, but neuroelectric signals are completely outside of cultural imprints and social conditioning; at that level, those lower functions cease to have meaning.

Telepathy is a phenomenon about which there is a lot of talk, but little understanding. Perhaps electromagnetic radiation between brains may explain certain aspects of neuroelectric telepathy, involving what is happening physically in the neural system as it is registered on the nerve endings and available for reception in another brain on the same "frequency," i.e. a brain that is operating on the same level and at the same speed (using "fast-moving, relativistic brain-waves" in Leary's parlance). Though it is a subject not taken seriously by the majority, it does seem that telepathy is a phenomenon that, given all the evidence, does seem to be occurring widely. Telepathy is not some mystical or occult mystery; for those who have experienced it, it is quite real and not at all otherworldly.

The Third Eye

As mentioned previously, the seventh "metaprogramming" circuit is often, and correctly, associated with what is known as the "third eye." This third eye is basically the seeing apparatus of the mind itself, and therefore ties in directly with what we have said about neuroelectric awareness. It is not precisely correct to say that consciousness of the third eye shows one the projector and screen of perception, but rather that the contents of that whole apparatus exist as a kind of creative, intelligent, novelty-generating system. Being aware of one's third eye is like being aware of the source of one's imagination; it is a virtually divine awareness. The third eye doesn't see for the mind; rather, it's that the mind exists fundamentally as a kind of eye, seeing its way through the twisting maze of perception and existence, always ready to provide new and more constructive perceptions—if it is allowed to operate freely.

Unfortunately, normal, everyday awareness tends to blot out one's awareness of these functions, as they are not immediately useful for survival in today's world. The stultifying influence of the dominant culture in the West definitely does not aid us here. But the good news is that this circuit is always operating in one's subconscious—thoughts of high quality bubble up all the time for many people. It's just that most of the time, one is not aware of the source of these thoughts, and one is not able to select from the range of alternatives that is the hallmark of true metaprogramming awareness. Don't be discouraged, though. Anyone can consciously metaprogram!

No Limits

According to John Lilly, *In the province of the mind, what one believes to be true is true or becomes true, within certain limits to be found experientially and experimentally. These limits are further beliefs to be transcended. In the mind, there are no limits.* Incidentally, this encapsulates what the esoteric traditions have always preached, and constitutes the 'final secret of the Illuminati': in the mind, *anything is possible.* There is in a very real sense no limit to what can potentially be thought; the possibilities are literally infinite. Neuroelectric metaprogramming can generate a multitude of thoughts around any situation or subject, and the hypothetical permutations for what thoughts can be generated about anything and everything are unlimited.

A key point of emphasis here is that fact that metaprogramming awareness gives one options and choices in a given situation that would, in ordinary consciousness, only be limited to one option with no understanding that the mind generated several *in potentia*. Naturally, this begins to border on the structure and function of the quantum wavefunction, but I shall refrain from getting too far afield here. Indeed, normally, as everyone knows, someone asks you a question and you reply with a single answer. You did not know that your mind had prepared several possibilities, and that, possibly, you could have selected a different one had you been privy to the information. With an active metaprogramming circuit, you are constantly aware of a number, a potentially substantial number, of perfectly appropriate and advantageous thoughts to accompany a given stimulus. Many have suggested that this type of awareness constitutes true free will, and that it undoubtedly exists, but is simply not exercised by the majority.

I'm not sure I would go that far, as I prefer to see metaprogramming as the essence of *true* will, rather than *free* will. The former concept goes a long way toward shedding some of the metaphysical baggage of any discussion of free will, and seems a better convention for describing the situation in a straightforward and empirical way. I will say that the spectral, multiple-choice reality of the seventh circuit does augment one's sense of freedom immeasurably. Indeed, it is liberating.

Neurological Relativity

The Einsteinian paradigm is embodied by and expressed through the neuroelectric metaprogramming circuit. It will be very difficult for me to translate what is experienced during this awareness of relativity, but I shall try to describe it anyway. Somehow, the "velocity" of the nervous system is accelerated to such a pitch during metaprogramming awareness that time dilation and mass-energy equivalence effects come fully to the fore of one's consciousness. If one is fully metaprogramming and has a clock handy, it is often fun to sit for a little while, relax a bit and then after a few minutes pose the question: When was the last time I looked at the clock? You make your guess, and let's say it's ten minutes. Well, you look back at the clock and a minute and a half have passed. Something has changed. In your reference frame, everything seems the same. But in some way, at this level of neuroelectric function, one's velocity relative to the standard reference frame has increased significantly. Time has apparently, and perhaps literally, slowed. This is the essence of special relativity.

Moreover, in this state one becomes acutely aware of the equivalence of mass and energy. It becomes readily apparent that mass is frozen energy, and energy is mass that has become dynamic. We might as well call the seventh circuit the "relativistic circuit," as it personifies the theory uncannily. All of this stands to some reason when we realize that the neuroelectric circuit is just that: an electrical neural circuit, or more precisely, the chemically and colloidally modulated electrical field making up our experience of mentation. Just what property of this electric field is "speeding up" to create the effects of time dilation is a mystery. But the fact that an electromagnetic field is being modulated and ramped up offers some hint that what is going on makes sense. That's about all I can say without urging the reader to aspire to his or her own neuroelectric awareness, where anyone with even a cursory knowledge of physics will recognize the functioning of this circuit as precisely relativistic. Don't knock it 'til you've tried it!

Leary's Light Beam

Leary gives an interesting take on Einstein's famous light-beam experiment. He of course reiterates the story of how Einstein, in coming to grips with the ideas that would later solidify into his famous special theory of relativity, imagined what it would be like actually to ride a beam of light. This, as is well-known, gave him historic insights. Leary goes on to point out that if Einstein were riding on a tram away from the local clock-tower at the speed of light, he would be riding on the same beam of light that left the clock-tower when the tram embarked. It is the very beam by which he can see what the clock reads. Of course, if this is the case, then the clock would appear frozen in place for as long as Einstein was travelling on the light beam! This is precisely what special relativity predicts will happen. As we speed up, time slows. If we are going at the speed of light (which for a massive object would be impossible, of course), time will have come to a stop in the external reference frame. In keeping up with the light beam emanating from the clock-tower, the clock can never have changed, and so it is fixed in place—along with the time it displays. In keeping up with the speed of light, the fictitious tram-rider has cut himself off from the passage of time.

The metaprogramming circuit, as its function increases in energy and intensity, somehow approaches the fundamental phenomenon of electromagnetic energy and as any psychonaut can tell you, time slows. It may be hypothesized that the nonlocal eighth circuit involves a transcendence of this barrier. More on that later!

Proficient Metaprogrammers

Seventh circuit awareness is most often found among advanced practitioners of yoga, mathematicians and physicists, many artists and musicians, and can be activated temporarily by psychedelic chemicals. Yoga, math, physics, art and music are all, in some sense, strivings after beauty and truth, and they are all activities in which one looks inward to find it. The first three types of people are actually doing activities, i.e. running programs, that could not function without some degree of metaprogramming awareness. Advanced meditation, advanced maths, and particularly relativity and quantum mechanics are all essentially metaprograms in themselves. Such activities lead very readily to seventh circuit awareness as they explicitly force one to partition one's consciousness, and keep everything straight, and it doesn't take long for people doing them to recognize their minds' rhythms and manipulate them. Many artists and musicians, though perhaps fewer per capita than the aforementioned groups, also develop a recognition of their brain's internal function from intensely looking inward—I believe the term is "soul-searching"—which, after all, is part of the job. I include writers under the term 'artists,' and of course we have the ultimate seventh circuit manual, *Alice's Adventures in Wonderland*, by the polymath adept Lewis Carroll. I suppose one could boil all this down to a more general definition, and point out that we may, perhaps, mean *metaprogramming proficiency* when we use the term *genius*. Such a person is one who has become so conscientious about his or her own thought processes that they begin to recognize the beat driving the music of mental consciousness. And one can ultimately play the beat, and consequently the music, however one wishes.

Seventh circuit adepts tend to find social fulfillment only in individuals of similar neurological capacity. There are not many equals around for metaprogramming geniuses; consequently many tend to prefer to be alone most of the time—rugged individualists who value their privacy. Surely some, however, like Leary or Wilson, are social butterflies. All are invisible to the majority.

Perception

Perception is a tricky subject. What we see, and experience in general, is not identical, and may really have very little to do with, that which is seen or experienced. As I have pointed out, everything we know is a process inside of our skulls. But this process is not strictly objective, at least at this level. The brain takes in raw sense data and is constantly constructing, editing, processing, evaluating all of it, and then delivering the result to our awareness. As Korzybski noted, whatever you say a thing is, it isn't. Not only that, but we get caught up in language games as well. Much of the time we're confusing reality and experience with linguistic conventions, and getting ourselves into quite a muddle. Suffice it to say, our experience of reality and reality itself are more often than not very far apart. Things get a little more unified, ideally, on the eighth circuit, but for now we have to realize that our "reality" is really an inner show of a gray, vibrating realm outside of our perception that is sending signals to us which our brains interpret into a tidy picture. Not only that, but the brain is constantly receiving signals we never know about, and generating output that usually remains subconscious. It is survivally beneficial to edit these signals out, and perhaps for various reasons we lack sensitivity as well. But the world and our brains are swirling with information to which we are, except when we attain seventh circuit awareness, quite oblivious. To become aware of this basic process is indeed the essence of metaprogramming.

Perspective

Trying to imagine metaprogramming awareness is like trying to imagine seeing three-hundred and sixty degrees all at once. It is to transcend spacetime and to transcend conventional modes of what we call perspective. Transitioning from the seventh to eighth circuits is like traveling on Einstein's famous beam of light. All time slows to a crawl and one can see, in one glorious moment, all that was, is and ever shall be. Space and time become exposed as fully relative, not only in the way we are used to—slowing or speeding time, bending or stretching space—but also with the realization that they are, in an objective sense, essentially arbitrary. Why do we have these four dimensions, just so? We tend to assume that all of existence, top to bottom, must have this feature. But why, really? As Dali was so fond of pointing out, spacetime is one among an infinite number of ways for existence and for perception to present themselves. And if the reader has not yet discovered Dali, a crime has been committed, and time is to be served looking deeply into his works. For fun, ask yourself how he saw the world, and if you find an answer, try to see it that way for a little while, too.

Transcending Ego

Metaprogramming awareness is really the way one transcends the ego and makes real choices. Most people are stuck in instinctive, unreflective robotism, and they don't even know it. This notion illustrates the essence of what has been meant when, in previous sections, the robotism of the human experience has been noted. Just looking at the word itself brings the picture somewhat into focus—we have our normal programming: our waking lives, our busy schedules, our normal tasks, our repetitive behaviors. When we have transcended this low order of awareness we have gone beyond—meta—our programming. Our ego-self is brought to our awareness by an artificial—false even—construct in our brain/mind apparatus which serves to keep us alive and breeding, at bottom. Negotiating terrestrial affairs without thinking too much about it—as thinking often destabilizes things—is a strategy that has worked for a long time; this is the ego's primary function.

Were one to have the audacity to rise above this robotic construct; to have the gall actually to attempt to reshape it, re-program it or transcend it altogether; one would be challenging, indeed, that which is expected of us, by our genes, possibly, and certainly by society—to mindlessly wade through the first, second, third and fourth circuit swamp. Challenging that accepted protocol has met with a lot of resistance, opposition and violence throughout all history. It is not for nothing that most people react with hostility to these ideas; the second-circuit ego is only used to dealing with its own territory, and when such unusual and ambiguous territory is presented, it often engenders fear, uncertainty and animosity. That such existential conservatism is so robotically hard-wired is a problem for the existentially adventurous or inquisitive, as they are in the minority and are not typically well-regarded.

In any event, it is the choice between robotism and the beginning of increased freedom; between the false self and the true self; between one choice and many choices; between habit and true will. Note that I do not use the term "free" will, but rather "true" will. It is not my intention to argue that we have a truly free and unconstrained will. However, metaprogramming awareness gives us access to avenues in our minds that may normally be hidden, and this augmented, more comprehensive will represents a truer and deeper version of ourselves, and is the product of self-realization. Therefore, the term 'true will' better approximates what is going on than the more loaded and ambiguous alternative. In any case, I wish more of us would rather live in truth than falsehood.

Many Worlds

Everett's Many-worlds interpretation of quantum mechanics recapitulates the seventh "meta-programming" circuit. The quantum mechanical wavefunction is a mathematical function that describes a quantum entity. That is, an entity in the quantum realm, like an electron. Naturally, the wavefunction can take on many different properties for a given quantum entity—potentially a very huge number. Say we're dealing with an electron. The Many-worlds interpretation stipulates that every potential electron, with each of the different possible properties, literally exists—each one in a separate universe! That is, the wavefunction predicts that an electron can have a velocity of one unit, or a velocity of two units, and each possibility has an appropriate probability of being measured. (The wavefunction gives us mathematical probabilities for certain things to occur). Well, the Many-worlds interpretation says that an electron with one unit of velocity, and an electron of two units of velocity, both exist at the same time in different "worlds," and if we measure a velocity of one in this universe, there is a universe next door, every bit as real as this one, in which a scientist, in the same situation, has just measured a velocity of two. This does away with the pesky "measurement problem" in quantum mechanics, in which it is impossible to define a measurement, because we don't know at what point the wavefunction collapses to give us a definite value of a measured variable.

This may all seem rather convoluted, but the point is that metaprogramming is a perfect analog for the MWI—each possible thought-stream, ready to fire and "collapse" into one neatly packaged result, is instead opened up into an array of possibilities from which to select. Through neuroelectric awareness, we become instantly cognizant of an array of different neurological pathways—or "universes"—and are able to go above and beyond the normal awareness of only one, i.e. only one choice, which isn't really a choice, with no knowledge that there were other fruitful paths our thoughts could take. In a way, with metaprogramming, we are given access to the un-collapsed wavefunction, and therefore given access to many different universes, each with its own possibilities.

Multiple-Choice

As I have pointed out, metaprogramming awareness occurs when consciousness gets channeled, in an uninhibited way, through the electric pathways of the brain. Upon activation, one becomes instantly cognizant of the numerous different routes thoughts can take, rather than the ordinary awareness of only one of them. And one even has some agency here. As I have noted previously, having seventh circuit awareness is like having access to the uncollapsed quantum wavefunction of the brain. Ordinarily, the wavefunction of the brain, in tandem with the neuroelectric circuit itself, will collapse itself into one eventuality for a unit of mental output. Decisions, discussions, opinions, personal thoughts, etc., etc. occur in this way for us, and we are wholly unaware of the bevy of alternative options that were being weighed in our subconscious. Well, when that subconscious process becomes conscious, we instantly have access to this higher-order process, and are able to "see" all of the other pathways before collapse takes place, which we are then able to consciously select. We have gone beyond our normal programming. Leary called this "multiple-choice," and that is precisely what it is.

Questions of free will remain murky, however. One is still reliant on the machinery of the brain at this level, and I have suggested that the term "true" will is more appropriate to describe the phenomenon than "free" will. Irrespective of all that, imprinting and experiencing full seventh circuit awareness for the first time is a personal revolution, and it is unforgettable. To keep active in this awareness requires presence, reflection, introspection, honest thought and some diligence—and it helps to have a good memory. But if you're reading this, chances are you're a metaprogrammer already, whether you know it or not!

Interpenetration

At the transition point with the eighth circuit, "outside" and "inside" cease to have well-defined meaning. Of course normally, we have external objects which are relatively autonomous but variable, and also, we ordinarily perceive ourselves—on the inside—as individual and invariable. At the transition point, this rigid dichotomy breaks down, and the reality of *process*—existence as a verb, rather than a noun—comes to the fore. Here, the object and the subject become equally invariable, and essentially one. The distinction between the personal self and the external reality breaks down, and one is no longer able to separate oneself from the world, or the world from oneself.

Of course, we read about this in the literature, and hear about it from the Buddhists and the Navajo, etc., but until one experiences it, one mustn't dismiss its reality and the awesomeness of the revelation. It is the basis for the famous symbol in Taoism of the yin and yang. Subject hooks with object, and object with subject, in an organic and completely holistic way. It is ultimate interpenetration.

Niels Bohr included a yin-yang symbol on his coat-of-arms, and for very good reason. In physics, the new reality is that the experimental apparatus, and that which it is measuring, cannot be meaningfully separated in any kind of coherent way mathematically. This is intimately related to Heisenberg's indeterminacy principle. The atoms in the apparatus have to interact, at a fundamental level, with the atoms or other particles being studied. And so, quantum mechanics takes that into account. Interpenetration is not only a mystical or philosophical principle; it is also a scientific one. As we shall see in the next section on circuit eight, quantum theory, despite the new age hooey, has a quite fundamental role at that level—the most fundamental level of our universe.

CIRCUIT 8

Indra's Net

This circuit is imprinted by extreme shock, "near-death" or "clinical death" experiences, out-of-body experiences, certain chemicals, etc. When this circuit is active, awareness has been rerouted to the nonlocal quantum information net, which happens to constitute the essence of all consciousness and is the basis for our universal reality. This is the universal wavefunction; the implicate order of Bohm; the infinite of the mystics. In a counter-intuitive fashion, this level gives rise to all other the other circuits, and informs and animates their existence.

At the level of dhyana, subject and object unify into one whole. Progressing to the level of samadhi — or rather circuit eight awareness — we see subject and object disappear altogether, leaving in their place pure "is-ness." At this level there is no such thing as distinction; there is but one universe, made of pure consciousness.

On the eighth circuit, inorganic matter is seen to be "alive." That is, the consciousness pervading nature, even down to individual atoms, is accessed and experienced. Atoms are not random entities; they are highly structured and ordered, and intelligent. How would chemistry be possible otherwise? The entire universe becomes one alive, aware being, each part being part of the whole, and the whole being made up of each part—none of which is extricable or extraneous. Indeed, the universe is not some cold, dead, random machine, but a living presence of unimaginable intelligence and complexity and subtlety. For those who have had it, this experience is unforgettable, indelibly pressed into one's soul, leading to a serenity and sensitivity that cannot be lost or forgotten. Once Indra's net catches you, it does not let go—but *you* must let go!

It has become clear that the nucleus of the atom comprises a complex organization of powerful interactions which operate according to harmonious relationships. Just as the DNA code, located in the nucleus of every cell, is the genetic brain which, via RNA, designs and manufactures bodies and nervous systems, so we can say that the nucleus of the atom contains or manifests the elemental "brain" which designs and constructs atoms and molecules, via perhaps the four fundamental forces, through the quantum language. Later on we shall explore the nature of this implicate order.

Universal Mind

The primary scientific advances of the twentieth century—those of relativity and quantum mechanics—frame, respectively, one's experience of awareness on the seventh and eighth circuits. The theories open up, in a dramatic vista, in a way that enables one's intellectual grasp of these concepts to become a fundamental consciousness. Suddenly they make perfect sense, and are wholly vindicated (experimentally, if one wishes). As far as I can tell, there is no scientific experience like it. It is a remarkable transition between third circuit rational symbolism, and the existential revolution that is the higher circuitry.

Here we have the high-energy, high-information language of the atomic electro-nucleus. Metaphysiological intelligence "integrates, engineers, organizes" atomic particles—creates, manipulates and coordinates atoms, and the entire dance of matter and energy in the universe. The energies which constitute every structure, every physical behavior, become available to the awareness. Everything—from atoms, to molecules, to DNA strands, to blood cells to neurons—is created and sustained by interacting quantum particles, be they photons, gravitons, gluons or W and Z bosons. A useful (if imprecise) analogy would be to say that these particles are like neurons in the universal brain that is the implicate order. These neurons send "signals" across time-spans of billionths-of-a-second and billions of years.

Activation

The higher circuits become activated (and potentially imprinted) when, simply enough, the power of the neural pathways, which are primarily electrical, increases to certain thresholds. Certain substances, as neurotransmitters, can artificially manipulate the electric highways of the nervous system into ratcheting the energy output to a sufficient level that latent potentials for consciousness become realized. Activation is, as previously stated, quite simply a matter of the level of power coursing through the nervous system. It would seem that ordinary neurotransmitters in the brain dampen its electromagnetic field, and that when certain measures are taken, or awareness affects the brain in a certain way, this electromagnetic flux increases to the point that new phenomena emerge consciously in the awareness. It is a decidedly open question what the nature of "natural" human awareness is, as most people reading these words have been raised in quite unnatural circumstances, using the conventional meaning of the word. Practices like Zen try to rediscover natural human awareness, and to what degree they succeed is probably quite variable. In any case, the circuits are there for the taking.

One

After initial energization of the neural highways, awareness of the body develops. As the degree of this synaptic flow increases, awareness has access to the DNA-RNA dialogue. Also, through metaprogramming, the nervous system imprints its own structure and operation as an electromagnetic transceiving instrument. Finally, one arrives at the experience of disembodied nonlocality, a quantum mechanical order that represents the consciousness of the universe, an experience that is frequently said to make the self "one with everything."

The body is directed and controlled by the brain. The brain has evolved through the intelligent unfolding of the DNA molecule, located in every cell of the body. The DNA molecule is composed of atoms that contain an even deeper intelligence—what we refer to as the implicate order—a universal mind, suffusing all matter and energy with an intelligence and a kind of inherent consciousness. The basic configuration of the entire universe finds itself in the all and the one via the nucleus of the atom, and its innate connection with all other nuclei. They could be likened to cosmic neurons within the universal nervous system. All of chemistry results from this dance of energy. This is the primary nature of the nonlocal quantum circuit.

Nonlocality

David Bohm, in the 1950s, predicted something called "nonlocality" in his formulation of quantum theory. John S. Bell, later on, proved that if the equations of quantum mechanics were internally consistent (and therefore correct), nonlocality would have to be a feature, which to many physicists then, and still today, is very unpleasant. *Technically*, what happens is that if two particles which share a quantum state—let's say two particles of light, or photons—are sent flying apart from one another, quantum theory predicts that their polarization angles—or simply, the orientations of the light particles—should be correlated in a way not predicted by classical, Newtonian physics. This is known as entanglement. And when experiments were run in the 1970s, by Clauser, Aspect and others, these correlations were found to exist, and quantum mechanics, *with* nonlocality, was preserved.

Non-technically, what this all means is that every particle in the universe is in some sort of universal (not local, nonlocal) linkage or communication with every other, instantaneously, everywhere. In other words, modern physics is telling us that everything is literally interconnected with everything else. Now, some people complain that the instantaneous "transmissions" between entangled particles violate relativity as they travel faster than light. The truth is, they *circumvent* relativity, as the two sets of functions are at different levels of nature. Relativity occurs at the level of mass and energy, space and time—the level of the seventh circuit. Quantum mechanics, entanglement, nonlocality occur at a more fundamental level—that level into which we are tuned by our eighth circuits. Indeed, the electromagnetic level involves transfers of *energy*. The quantum level involves transfers of *information*. When one recognizes that different rules apply to different semi-autonomous levels of nature, there need be no conflict. And tuning into this nonlocal information "field" uncovered by Bell's Theorem is what circuit eight consciousness is all about.

The Fundamental Infinite

Quantum, neuro-atomic consciousness involves the direct awareness of the objective nature of the wavefunction along with its properties of charge and spin, the information field behind the forces of electromagnetism and gravitation, and the stark reality of entanglement and nonlocality that have been long promised by the Schrödinger Equation. Subatomic nuclear energy becomes a subjective experience. These forces, with which one comes to identify fundamentally, are those which have brought particles, atoms, molecules, cells, nervous systems and solar systems into existence. It is at this ontological stage that the platitude "being one with everything" has its root. Post-physiological consciousness in the individual is identical with the forces which construct stars, let them burn, finally go supernova, and collapse into black holes. It is, in a way, the nervous system of the universe. For the psychonaut who experiences this level of reality, the pleasure is astronomical. This is the infinite.

It is a possibility that the external technological manifestations of eighth circuit awareness would involve mastery of the principles of both nuclear fusion and gravitational fields, which might entail the scientific mastery of singularity. Obviously, a technological development along these lines could only happen a very great distance in the future, and it is the present author's belief that humanity will be so transformed by the time of such developments as to make it impossible still to call the agents of these changes "human." It is quite possible that one major goal of any intelligence that reaches this level of sophistication might be to explore and crack the secrets of black holes, as they are the most mysterious, vexing, and potentially the most consequential subject-objects in the universe.

The Future of the Past

It is my impression that many if not most aboriginal peoples had at least some direct awareness of quantum nonlocality, and that this manifested for them as an organic concomitance of their undivided existence—ecologically, socially, culturally and individually. Far from being a circuit that had not evolved into existence yet, this awareness was a natural part of the human continuum, and awareness of its function was perfectly necessary. Native peoples did not see this as a circuit, but their famously mystical notions about how humans tie into the ecosystem, and how all Earth is one indivisible being, with a spirit—a kind of consciousness—illustrate that it could have been no other type of awareness that brought these beliefs and spiritual practices into being.

North American Indians, for example, knew quite a bit more about the workings of the noosphere than a businessman in Manhattan, yet we have this stubborn tendency to posit that they were primitive and could not possibly have been sophisticated enough to have known about phenomena of awareness that we have begun to *re*-discover in the twentieth century. As I argue, these higher circuits are not about the future, but about the present, and potentially the anthropological past. We tend to be very chauvinistic in believing that the present must be superior in every way to all past periods, but civilization is extremely complex, and there have been, undoubtedly, some retrogressive trends in several areas when it comes to disconnected, sedentary living. There is also more to say about the belief in man's destiny pertaining to space migration, which some authors claim is driving the evolution of the higher circuits into existence for a future away from Earth. Suffice it to say that it has become clear that man's destiny lies not in *his* future in space, but that of his evolutionary offspring. The higher circuits are here, now, and while future evolution would doubtless utilize the physical processes that give rise to them, they are every bit as much a part of man's subconscious *today*.

Next Steps

The "higher" neurological circuits are actually inherent. That is, they involve a redirection of consciousness through pathways in the fabric of the cosmos itself. That is, they are actually fundamentally extant in matter, energy, and information. They are not developing along genetic evolutionary lines; they have been there all along. It may, of course, be the next step in Earth evolution to stress them in significant numbers, but man's future is still very much an open question. Higher circuits do not become active when genetic circuits light up, so much as they respond to higher and higher levels of energy coursing through the nervous system. One's awareness enters the seventh circuit when the neuro-electric threshold has been reached. This has to do with a redirection of awareness through electrical pathways in the brain; one becomes aware on the eighth circuit when one accesses the quantum subrealm and taps into the nonlocal field of the universe. Somehow, all of this comes about through ascending energy levels in the nervous system, although it is a total mystery at this point how this works, scientifically. The important point is that these circuits are not evolutionary but rather natural and inherent to the physical structures and functions of the human nervous system. Nature doesn't need to evolve functions that already exist. Utilize them in more ingenious ways, yes.

Preview of the Implicate Order

Bohm's "implicate order" (and more technically his "quantum potential") recapitulates the eighth "nonlocal quantum" circuit. Quantum mechanics is a tricky business. We have discussed the wavefunction a little bit, which is usually understood through the "Copenhagen interpretation." This is a different, and more mainstream, interpretation than the Many-worlds one. In the Copenhagen interpretation, the wavefunction is in a state known as "superposition" before a measurement is made. That is, it's in sort of a mysterious, ambiguous state in which no outcome is favored over any other. When we make a measurement, the superposed wavefunction "collapses" into one definite, explicit outcome.

This has weird features. One of which is that collapse occurs everywhere all at once. That is, if you had, say, a laboratory on the moon, and you're doing some quantum experiments, something strange is going on in a laboratory on Earth with whom you are collaborating. When the wavefunction collapses in your laboratory on the moon, it instantaneously collapses in the Earth lab, as well. Why is this strange? Because it violates the theory of relativity. You can communicate your results only at the speed of light. But in reality, as soon as the wavefunction collapsed on the moon, it collapsed at precisely that instant on Earth as well. Some "force," traveling infinitely quickly—faster than the speed of light—collapsed that wavefunction on Earth as well. This ambiguous, faster-than-light behavior, is known as nonlocality. For Bohm, this was inherent in the nature of the wavefunction. His "Bohmian mechanics"—yet another interpretation of quantum mechanics—has it that there are things called "hidden variables" determining the behavior of quantum systems, and that they are beyond our ability to measure at this time. He posited that, despite the fact that quantum particles seem to have discontinuous histories, they actually have continuous histories in higher dimensions. His interpretation was the first serious version of quantum mechanics to embrace nonlocality, which he had mixed feelings about, but felt was unavoidable.

It has been confirmed through experiment that John Bell, and his famous theorem, are correct in that nonlocality is real and unavoidable if we are to accept the theoretical premises of quantum mechanics unambiguously. This is exhibited in a property known as "entanglement," in which correlated particles are shown to retain their correlations in a way that classical theory cannot predict, and that we now readily observe. Nonlocality and entanglement are physical realities that are at the heart of the "quantum circuit," and this is the arena into which our awareness feeds when we reach this level beyond metaprogramming. Physics has mapped our deepest subconscious, and hopefully our future, as well.

Nietzsche's Superman

Quite interestingly, Nietzsche emphatically did not mean for his concept of the "superman" to be construed as an evolutionary phenomenon. That is, he felt not that biological evolution would generate supermen, but the self-realization of the right type of man would. This of course implies, as I have laid out, that the higher circuits are not precisely evolved functions, but rather inherent in the structure and subconscious behavior of the nervous system. This is a matter of great confusion. Many writers have argued that this phenomenon is a genetic one, and that we are all dynamically evolving, over the generations, toward a beast that is superior for his chromosomes. This is not at all what Nietzsche meant. He was quite explicit that many figures in the past could serve as models for his superman, such as Caesar or Christ, and clearly, persons two thousand years in the past do not represent an evolutionary step forward. Nietzsche well understood the phenomena of the higher circuits, and whether he was aware of it or not, portions of his writings are direct transmissions from this higher consciousness. He was, in his own way, an example of the type of which he spoke. Is Nietzsche the unique species toward which humanity is evolving? Or was he a self-realized, exceptional individual... human?

Quantum Consciousness

Nothing becomes everything on the quantum circuit. Void becomes infinity. The phantoms that seem not to exist objectively outside of your skull are at once made real. Until one imprints this circuit, the only major realization can be yoga—union. Reality can only be experienced as yin and yang—outside and inside are complementary and neither can exist without the other. Later on, this duality disappears completely. One is left with infinities within infinities, and objective and subjective are wholly indistinct; any division between the two means nothing. In samadhi, there is paradoxically both a supreme connection with, and total severance from, the body. The mystics have been reporting from this state for thousands of years, and what they were really describing, in language that seems woefully inadequate, was the reality that we now know underlies the entanglement and associated nonlocal "field" uncovered by modern science. As time goes on, perhaps we can get a firmer handle on just what all this means scientifically, and potentially existentially as well. It is a possibility that, if quantum computers are set up in the proper way, this circuit may inform an incipient consciousness for A.I. machines, or entities. Time will tell. Engineering based upon the dynamics of this realm will guide the future of technology, and the future of man. Knowledge of all this is still very much in its infancy, but things change, and get more interesting all the time....

The Ground

We all know at this point that the basic behavior of our universe is governed essentially by particles interacting at the atomic level. Physics, chemistry and biology all point so directly at this truth that it would be ridiculous at this point to assume it to be spurious. All of the objects in explicate reality, our bodies and brains are composed of atoms. What many do not know is that matter and energy are not the fundamental realities of nature. What many further do not know is that consciousness can be directed, through the nervous system, into the ground of this atomic realm, opening up objective reality and demonstrating, to those who have discovered it, that reality is ultimately "made" of consciousness — some say mind or spirit. This is the most fundamental and highest dimension of our universe, beyond space and time, and it would seem rather foolish to assume that there could not be dimensions beyond it. In any case, though it seems that matter and energy rule the day, and that's it, the reality is that we are all ultimately composed of and animated by a ground that is common to both. This is the implicate order of Dr. Bohm, and the nonlocal quantum circuit of which we speak.

THE IMPLICATE ORDER

The Implicate Order, The Nonlocal Circuit, Consciousness

David Bohm's hypothesis of the implicate and explicate orders is particularly relevant to the themes of this book. So much so that I have decided to devote a section to it and related matters. It deals in turn with the subject of locality and nonlocality, the collapse of the wavefunction, the objectivity of the wavefunction, what may potentially be the nature of consciousness, and quantum theory as a method of describing how the ground of implicate prespace unfolds into the explicate structures of spacetime—instead of the dominant assumption that natural structures and forces are based fundamentally upon the interactions of particles and fields. This may seem rather abstract, but hopefully as we go along the interested reader will acquire a feel for it, if he or she doesn't have one already.

The implicate order, also known as the "enfolded" order, comprises the fundamental order or ground of reality, out of which the explicate order—space, time, force, matter and energy—unfolds. Appropriately, the explicate order is also called the "unfolded" order. Originally, this schema was created in order to explain the erratic and discontinuous behavior of particles in the subatomic realm. It was happily discovered subsequently that it is a highly useful philosophical principle for a number of reasons. With the implicate order, space and time are no longer seen as the ultimate bedrock of reality, but rather sub-forms which arise from a ground that is common to them and to all of the matter and energy within them. In other words, the implicate order is the ground from which reality emerges. Objects are seen to have only a limited degree of autonomy and stability.

Objects separated by great distances in space (the explicate order) are, in this scheme, seen to be directly correlated and in constant interrelationship in the implicate order. This is where, in quantum theory, entanglement comes in. Thus, every particle, every physical object in explicate reality is in some kind of nonlocal relationship with every other. This is our nonlocal, quantum *eighth circuit*. Consciousness enters, necessarily, because in each moment, content that was previously implicate unfolds into an explicate awareness, and content that was once explicate, re-folds into the implicate order. In other words, consciousness is the implicate order, and the explicate order comprises the contents of that consciousness.

There seems to be confusion about whether quantum entanglement violates the special theory of relativity and whether this amounts to a major, jarring conflict in our theory. If one assumes that the level at which entanglement occurs is more fundamental than the plane of mass-energy, there need be no conflict. Matter and energy are deep, but not fundamental. That is, we can abstract relatively autonomous sub-wholes or sub-levels from nature. Classical mechanics would be a sub-whole that is limited in relation to quantum mechanics, which is a more comprehensive sub-totality. Similarly, electromagnetism is a less fundamental sub-whole than the nonlocal circuit, which is its ground and is what informs and really gives life to it. It is no coincidence that in a precisely analogous way, the neuroelectric circuit is a relatively autonomous sub-totality in its own right, that is underlain by the quantum circuit with its dynamics as given by the implicate order hypothesis. It is worth noting that light defines space and time. Space and time would have no meaning for us outside of the phenomenon of electromagnetic radiation. When you've gone deeper than light, you've gone completely beyond and outside of space and time. This is the reality of the implicate order.

Consequently, it is perfectly possible to transmit *information* faster than light—the process doesn't depend on electromagnetism. It does seem to be impossible to transmit mass-energy faster than light. So relativity has its place. According to Dr. Bohm, from the point of view of the implicate order, the formative fields at the foundation of reality comprise a set of potentialities, and in each moment there's a selection for a particular potential to be realized depending to some extent on past history, and to some extent on creativity. The implicate order is like an artist with a photographic memory. The creativity inherent in nature mirrors the creativity of the unfettered human mind. In reality, the phenomena are identical.

I do not feel that consciousness has to be expressed as human beings; in fact, I feel even a rock has a very low order of consciousness, because the implicate order informs every atom and gives it a sense of objective being. The permutations for consciousness are infinite.

The Cosmic Hologram

The holographic principle restores objectivity and order to a universe from which quantum mechanics (or its most popular interpretations) takes it away. The cosmic hologram encodes all of reality on its surface, so anything not under the act of observation still exists implicitly. The Copenhagen interpretation posits that anything not under observation at best cannot be said to have any real or concrete features and at worst doesn't even properly exist. The implicate order which comprises the cosmic hologram allows things to exist independently of an active observer. While to say that something has no independent existence outside of perception is a fruitful and useful philosophy up to a point, reality in fact goes beyond it and back toward reason.

Given the fact that the cosmic hologram has a specific set of programming, objectivity and reasonableness are quite safe in reality. Nonlocality allows one to metaprogram the directives of the hologram. There is also the fact that in each part of the universe the whole is contained. This is a common experience of many yogis and psychonauts. If you have a photographic plate encoding a hologram, each region of the plate contains the information and potential capacity to project the entire three-dimensional image of the hologram. Each small region contains the whole and undivided portion of the full hologram. Analogously, at every point of spacetime, the implicate order enfolds the information for the entire explicate order, just as every cell in an organism contains the DNA instructions of the entire macroscopic organism.

Physicists, particularly string theorists, have, in the last few decades, come to believe that the entire universe may literally be a hologram projected from its boundary. The mathematics of black holes have led some to feel that a volume of space can be thought of as encoded on a lower-dimensional boundary of that volume. The entropy relations of black hole physics indicate this to be a real phenomenon. This confluence of the notions of the implicate-explicate orders and gravitational physics is interesting, and perhaps there is a meaningful isomorphism there. Certainly, positing the implicate order as especially similar to a hologram, and positing that the universe may literally be a hologram, is suggestive and it is encouraging that such ideas may have appreciable merit.

Collapsing into the Explicate

I feel very strongly that Bohm's implicate order describes consciousness so well because it *is* consciousness. I.e., the nonlocal quantum circuit is both the ground of mass-energy and the source of consciousness. I see both mass-energy and mind as extensions of or projections from this ground of active information. Therefore, I like to separate mind and consciousness. I feel that mind is an approximately classical, neurological-biological construction, and that consciousness is a quantum phenomenon. Explicate-implicate. Matter and energy are explicate as well, and in my opinion not as fundamental as the quantum ground from which they arise. It appears to me that mass-energy is at the level, internally and perceptually, of the (classical) neuro-electric network giving rise to all functions of the brain, such as memories, thoughts, emotions, etc., and that one transcends both matter and mind, or in other words the function of the brain (and potentially the speed of light barrier) when one crosses to the fundamental nonlocal, quantum consciousness. This has a correlate with the ego as well. The ego can be seen as a classical, mechanistic construct of the mind which, when transcended, transforms into the "true self" which is a primary objective.

Conscious activation of the eighth circuit manifests as the direct physical manifestation of the wavefunction. Superposition and collapse, entanglement and nonlocality. One can actually witness the very fundament of the quantum theory one has learned about and struggled to understand, in a kind of psychonautical, participatory vista. This awareness, which is unmistakable, supports Bohm's notions and Many-worlds more than it does the Copenhagen interpretation. I do mention superposition and collapse here, and it does go on—in a way. But not in such a fragmented fashion as we are taught at university. There is never a sharp division between superposition and collapse; it is rather one undivided, flowing movement, and there is an interplay between the implicate and explicate orders. The implicate order is the mind of nature, an inherent, eternal consciousness that is always complexifying and, in a sense, learning. The explicate is what unfolds out of it, and it is at this junction between implicate and explicate that confusion arises. The process by which structures arise out of the ground involves what we think of as "collapse," but in reality there is never any discontinuity. Just constant change. This becomes a felt, visceral, conscious reality during eighth circuit imprinting and awareness. The wavefunction appears, not as an abstraction, but as an objective, alive presence, and theory is laid out before one unforgettably. That is, one can't forget the character of the experience. Quantifying one's findings into advanced maths is another matter!

Tunnels

The implicate, conscious ground "collapses" into mass-energy at every point of spacetime, over and over, billions of times a second, giving rise to the explicate structures of Nature which, as a result of this fact, are only relatively invariant but are at a finer level undergoing a rapid, constant rate of change. This is mirrored in the interface between human consciousness and the human mind, in which the quantum circuit informs neuroelectricity in every instant, superposing as a set of different possible choices or mindsets, which collapse during a conscious event of perception into a given awareness or state of mind. So we can see there is a real oneness between the consciousness of Nature itself, and also the primate mind. In truth, it is only one process.

As for consciousness, it occurs to me that if particles can tunnel through space, they must also be able to tunnel through time. It further occurs to me that consciousness may, at least in part, be the result of such quantum tunneling through time. This must be some sort of abstract definition of entanglement, which seems to be akin to a process that enables information to tunnel through time. Naturally, the wavefunction of the brain distributes entangled brain states across the neuroelectric pathways, and perhaps this tunneling analogy is a constructive way to think about it.

Awareness Unfolding

I'd like to make a few more points before moving on. It is apparent that there are both local and nonlocal elements governing our consciousness. We can be consumed by the overpowering oneness of the universe upon the ignition of a higher state of mind, and we can also be forgetful old farts. We can have brains constituted of a holographic phenomenon (in which each part contains the whole), and we can suffer crippling brain damage. The brain's neuroelectric dance relies for its operation on nonlocal quantum phenomena as well as local "classical" ones. The brain correlate of one's conscious experience is an electromagnetic excitation. The entire EM field of the brain can be likened to an implicate order distributed over the whole brain providing the basis for the contents of mental consciousness.

But after all, the brain does not constitute our fundamental nature. As Philip K. Dick pointed out, consensus reality can almost be seen as an epiphenomenon of the deeper, truer nonlocal reality. The explicate order is a construct, and while it is real, it often diverts one's attention from the true unfolding of nature, unless one knows how to look. One of the best things a human can do is to stop, take a breath and reflect. Resonance with the harmony of nature can illustrate the rhythm of the implicate-explicate interchange powerfully, but too often we're distracted.

Some people who tune into that resonance feel that nature could be nothing other than designed by a higher being or force. While that may ultimately be true, I feel the implicate order of nature is an independent one, unfolding out of a dual-principle of necessity *and* contingency. It would be better to describe the universe, not as based upon a principle of intelligent design, but rather as based upon a principle of intelligent *unfolding*. The truth here, as ever, is extremely subtle.

Part of that subtlety is the fact that subatomic particles are not the primary determinants of the behavior of the universe, as is so commonly assumed, but rather they lie at the ever changing boundary between matter and consciousness—a suffusing consciousness that is the root of nature, and all of the particles in it. The quantum theory that has developed over the last hundred years in fact indicates, if one knows how to look properly, that these classical "billiard-ball" notions of the Cartesian-Newtonian materialist mindset are woefully insufficient to explain the true fundamental behaviors we have discovered—and are therefore false. Really, we know this, and the vast majority have failed to catch up to the more holistic (and correct) paradigm. Physicists like Henry Stapp and Richard Muller are doing their job to try to convince people of the reality of the new physics, and their language is positively marvelous.

Another facile assumption the dogmatic materialists make is that we live in a cold, dead, random, meaningless universe. I, for one, feel sorry for them. Why do they not see intelligence and order in an atom? An atom is certainly not a random entity! It is extraordinarily complex, and engages in a subtle, beautiful dance, making possible everything you see, including that face in the mirror. How everything can be considered a total accident makes very little sense. There is order and beauty everywhere one looks. But once again, we're always distracted, usually by trivialities.

One must realize that one is a participant in a nontrivial process, and the degree to which one appreciates it is the degree to which one's life will have high quality. We feel we are disconnected, and that could be the result of a slew of factors that would be outside the scope of this book to discuss. It helps to remember that for the most part we are neither observing detachedly from the outside, nor creating freely from the inside, but rather *participating*. The greater recognition and willingness we apply to our participation is directly proportional to the degree that we are really living.

TO CONCLUDE

The End

To me, the term "spirituality" refers to how one fits into the universe (or multiverse). A person or people with a higher degree of spirituality can be said to be more intimately tied to the workings of nature, or even to those beyond nature, potentially. This book is presented in an orderly way, and makes much reference to scientific principles, but it is also a deeply spiritual book. Indeed, it seeks to formulate and specify precisely what is occurring to people during what can often be called spiritual experiences. It is my hope that I have provided a map, or guide, to those who are interested in seeking the truth, both of nature, and of the self. In doing so, I am also hopeful that I have shown that the two phenomena are really one. If you can walk away from this book feeling that the light reflecting from the page and hitting your eye is not ordinary, then I am happy. And if you have learned that the deepest secrets of the universe exist within you, and that you have access to them, then my wish to write this book was not in vain. You realize, you understand. The meaning of existence — is existing.

APPENDIX

A Quantum Mechanical Interpretation of the Eight Circuit Model

One day a few years ago it dawned on me that the wavefunction of quantum mechanics can be considered as a "mandala," if you will, representing the top two echelons of the Eight Circuit Model: the seventh "metaprogramming" circuit and the eighth "nonlocal" circuit. This will be seen to validate Robert Anton Wilson's amendment of the original theory whereby he transposed the sixth and seventh circuits, elevating the metaprogramming circuit's position in the scheme. I am not aware of his reasons for this change, and the following may have been a subconscious or possibly even conscious motivation for him.

Basically, metaprogramming awareness can be visualized in the wavefunction as an inward compression of the x-axis, which represents spacetime values, toward the y-axis, which represents the probability of finding a given object with an array of particular characteristics at a particular spacetime value. Once the compression is complete and all the values of x have been squeezed in and lie on the y-axis, every state or possibility under consideration of the object's function has a 100% probability of occurring—

simultaneously. This can be considered as an abstract definition of the type of consciousness dubbed by Lilly "metaprogramming."

As for the nonlocal eighth circuit, we shift our focus toward the perpendicular dimension of the graph which stands for $\Psi(x,y,z,t)$, the probability of finding a particle with particular characteristics at a particular spacetime value. As before, we shall see what happens when there is a compression, this time of Ψ values, but as the wavefunction is not symmetric about the x-axis as it was about the y-axis, there are now two degrees of freedom rather than one: Ψ can either go downward or upward. But if this happens, the consequence is that unity no longer equals one! If the universe is truly nonlocal in nature at the microscopic level, this stands to reason.

For if one no longer equals itself, then the one and the many or the one and the fractions (pieces) of the whole are identical.

Even stranger, if somehow the value of Ψ drops to zero, $1=0$. Interpret this scenario as you will. Some suggestions of lines of thought are: infinity (or transfinity) equals nothing, unity is void, equilibrium (balance) defines wholeness, and so on.

As I have never encountered this particular analogy before, I hope it is not unreasonable. It is a rather unusual way to think about the wavefunction, and does not follow mathematical procedure, but as a kind of generalized metaphor, it seems fruitful and useful, at least in conceptualizing what may be happening in an abstract way. I hope you agree.

ABOUT THE AUTHOR

James A. Heffernan is relatively new to the writing scene, but feels his unique perspective on the nature of reality can enlighten and inspire all readers and provide them with the sense that there is much more to human existence than meets the eye. This is an existence that, he feels, is anything but banal and boring, as his work is designed to show. He studied physics and anthropology at the University of Utah, focusing especially on the foundations of the new physics on the one hand, and on the psychology of aboriginal hunter-gatherers on the other—having hardly suspected that he would find meaningful parallels between the two. In 2016 he authored his first book, *The Reality of Hunter-Gatherers*. James is also a published poet who feels a profound sense of satisfaction in the degree of focus, through the mysteries of the creative impulse, that a properly executed poem can bring forth. In all his writing, he writes from the soul, and hopes the reader appreciates the connection.

New Falcon Publications
Publisher of Controversial Books and CDs
Invites You to Visit Our Website:
http://www.newfalcon.com

At the Falcon website you can:

- Browse the online catalog of all our great titles, including books by Robert Anton Wilson, Christopher S. Hyatt, Israel Regardie, Aleister Crowley, Timothy Leary, Osho, Lon Milo DuQuette and many more
- Find out what's available and what's out of stock
- Get special discounts
- Order our titles through our secure online server
- Find products not available anywhere else including:
    - One of a kind and limited availability products
    - Special packages
    - Special pricing
- And much, much more

NEW FALCON PUBLICATIONS

Get online today at http://www.newfalcon.com